SUBURBIA
I SURVIVED, SO CAN YOU.

SHARON RADCLIFF

iUniverse, Inc.
New York   Bloomington

Suburbia
I Survived, So Can You.

iUniverse books may be ordered through booksellers or by contacting:

iUniverse
1663 Liberty Drive
Bloomington, IN 47403
www.iuniverse.com
1-800-Authors (1-800-288-4677)

Because of the dynamic nature of the Internet, any Web addresses or links contained in this book may have changed since publication and may no longer be valid. The views expressed in this work are solely those of the author and do not necessarily reflect the views of the publisher, and the publisher hereby disclaims any responsibility for them.

ISBN: 978-1-4502-2645-5 (sc)
ISBN: 978-1-4502-2646-2 (ebook)

Printed in the United States of America

iUniverse rev. date: 10/05/2010

Dedicated to my children, who brighten my every day

Table of Contents

Acknowledgments

I want to thank the many people who helped make this book a reality, from the multitude of friends we made in New Jersey who ultimately made it feel like home to the editors, proofreaders, friends, and family who read over the manuscript and made sure it was fit to print. I love writing, but you all helped me turn my dreams and visions into a tangible result.

I especially want to thank my husband and children for their love and support, and for allowing themselves to be the subject of this book. Okay, my children are a bit young to give me their formal permission, but I hope they forgive me when they get a bit older for sharing our experiences together. As always, I want to thank my parents, sisters, and brothers for giving me strong roots and a courageous soul so I can go out there and experience what life has to offer. I also need to thank my in-laws for managing to be so wonderful that I can't relate to in-law horror stories whenever I hear them.

A special thank you to my illustrator, Neil Kleid, who did a fantastic job bringing some of the ideas in this book to life.

And so I present to you, with much fanfare and hoopla, my latest creation, hot off the press, *Suburbia: I Survived, So Can You*. If you can't relate, and suburbia is a place you've never been and never plan on going, if you prefer skyscrapers to strip malls and cars to deer, then please forgive me for telling my little tale of how a city girl found herself lost one day in suburbia, and try to get in a few laughs while you read my story.

Introduction:
How This Book Came to Be

I've wanted to write a book about suburbia for a long time, but my husband was not in the least bit enthralled with the idea. After all, I'm a city girl, born and bred. What did I know about Costco and Target, Mommy and Me classes and playdates? Even Pathmark was a new phenomenon for me. He did not want me to make us look bad; or more specifically, make him look bad. It was one thing if I messed up my own life, but he was less than thrilled with anything that affected him. He simply wanted to be a private man and have a nice private life on a quiet street in suburbia without me plastering our every mishap and adventure on paper for the entire world to see. However, once I get an idea in my head, I get so excited that it's like a fly in my bedroom on a warm summer night; it doesn't go away. So the book was written, and the book is here. (You're reading it, aren't you?)

So how did this book come about? Well … he finally agreed. After much pleading and convincing and a few rereads to make sure he wouldn't be totally humiliated and forced to run out of town with a paper bag over his head, he allowed this book to come to fruition.

After much sweat and tears, I present to you *Suburbia: I Survived, So Can You.*

Suburbia is a place where you have to get into a car to get your morning milk, and if you want to find another human to converse with, you just may have to join a Mommy and Me (more on this later), but it's also a place where you can finally find more than two blades of grass in a row, and your neighbors seem to want to get to know you and bring over fresh-baked brownies when you move in and more batches when you come home from the hospital with a new baby. All this instead of what typically happens in the city, where neighbors will come over to you on the day you're moving out and, standing directly in front of your moving truck, innocently ask, "Hi, are you new in the neighborhood?" when you've been there for five years. Suburbia, a place where your children will be able to get up close and personal with rabbits, chipmunks, and magnificently-colored birds right in your own backyard without having to make a trip to the zoo, a place that despite the routines, carpools (more on this later, too!), and lack of grocery stores on every corner, you may come to find your own personal inner peace.

Out in suburbia, away from the endless noise and manic pace of city life, you may finally have time to think and slow down enough to smell the roses. It's a place that, despite its hair-raising commitment to calmness and order, you may one day finally call home.

1

House Shopping

We didn't initially start looking for a house in New Jersey. It was only after many weeks of house shopping in Queens, the neighborhood where we were living at the time, with the plan that we'd buy there and my husband would continue to commute to New Jersey for work, that the thought emerged that maybe if we moved out to the suburbs, our dollar would take us a little farther, and we could actually get a few blades of grass thrown in for our hard-earned dough. It took some convincing and the realization that there was nothing worthwhile on the market in Queens before I was ready to venture a look at—might I say it—suburbia.

People spoke of New Jersey as if it would solve all of life's problems. They talked about eighty-by-one-hundred-foot lot sizes; I was used to thinking in units of eighteen by twenty-five, and I couldn't comprehend what a lot that big would look like. Maybe if I knocked down six houses in a row on my street in Queens, I could begin to come up with a lot size that big. I tried to imagine a house as big as the school on the next block or the park I used to play in as a child and couldn't believe such a thing actually existed. Being a born and bred city girl, used to houses that were so close together that when my neighbor opened his fridge, I could tell him he was low on milk, I found this amount of property allotted per house too strange to be true. They indulged our fantasies, talking about houses in New Jersey that were built on an acre of land, while I was ready to put down my life savings for a shoebox. "New Jersey," they said with long, satisfied sighs. "It's like wonderland, a place where dreams come true." They said that in New Jersey you could have a lawn in the front *and* the back of your house. In Queens we would pretend to have a front lawn and would try to picnic on our four-by-four-foot plot of land, but the picnic blanket would be hanging over the sidewalk and the walkers-by thought they could share our bourekas with us. In New Jersey, they said, you could have a swimming pool and even a tennis court on your property; that's how big the lots were. It made me wonder, *If it's so great, how come they don't live there?* But first let's flash back to my initial days house shopping in Queens that led up to the big move.

My husband and I started out on the first of what I imagined would probably be many Sundays looking at houses for sale. Our first step was the neighborhood real estate agency. The only woman inside, whom I presumed to be a real estate agent, looked pleasant enough and asked us what we were looking for. Well, that was the first problem, as my husband and I wanted exactly the opposite things. I said, "A house," and he said, "A two-family" at precisely the same time. Then we both proceeded to explain ourselves. I liked the privacy of a semi- or fully-detached house, and my husband liked the benefits of renting the top floor and having the extra income to help pay our mortgage. After we decided we'd look at both, her next question was, "How much are you willing to spend?" This time I jumped in really fast and said my figure, which of course was way too low for the market, and from the look on our real estate agent's face, for any market since World War II. She began telling us about open houses in the neighborhood that she thought we should look at. We took a bunch of different scraps of paper containing addresses and were on our way.

The first house—if you could call it that—we looked at was a semi-detached house. It was so old, I expected a two-hundred-year-old man to pop out of one of the rooms and begin giving us a tour.

The carpet was shredded, the furniture was turn of last century, the bathroom was Gummy Bear pink and black; the house should have been torn down two hundred years ago, and they were selling this little eighteen-foot-wide space for $650,000. I would take it off their hands for a dollar—I'd even do them a favor and pay the taxes.

I know you need to have vision with some of these properties to see their potential, but this was requiring something closer to prophecy. And where did they get the nerve to charge these prices? Ten years ago I could have bought three of these houses for that price, and now they act like they did you a favor if they sold you one. (Did I tell you that the agent informed us the price was non-negotiable?) But that's how it is; we all know at least three houses we could have bought twenty years ago for $250,000 and now they're selling for a million, and we all sit and tell our stories to anyone who will listen as if the mere telling will make the houses ours.

The second house we visited was a townhouse, attached on both sides (suburbia was looking more appealing by the minute), and the whole family, including grandparents, aunts, uncles, and cousins, were over for the afternoon occupying the various rooms, each engaged in different activities, making it feel as if you were on the set of some television show. It seemed like the family members were all given roles or scripts to make the house look as warm and wonderful as possible. *If they were so comfortable and having such a good time there,* I wondered, *why were they putting it up for sale?* The grandfather, or what appeared to be the grandfather, was sitting on a rocking chair when we walked in, all smiles. In the living room was a big spread of drinks and cake, and a few family members were involved in an afternoon tea. Upstairs some girls were busy in what appeared to be a makeshift gym. There were a few men engaged in a very boisterous conversation off in another room. Too bad the people didn't come with the house because they looked like they were having more fun than I was. All in all, the house was quite small, but they were asking almost seven hundred thousand dollars for it. No wonder they all looked so happy; they were going to take the money they would make from the sale of the house and buy themselves a sprawling mansion somewhere in the Midwest or the South, and the joke would be on us.

My husband is a tall man, which is wonderful if you need someone to get down some dishes from a high cabinet, or change a light bulb when you don't have a stool nearby, but when it comes to buying a house in the city, this suddenly is no longer such a great commodity. In some houses, he would never be able to go into the basement. In others, he would have to hunch every time he used the staircase, so we were naturally ecstatic when the next house we looked at was advertised as having tall ceilings.

I already knew from my previous two experiences not to get my hopes up too high and wasn't expecting to walk into the White House or the Sistine Chapel, but I was expecting something that resembled a tall ceiling. The lady showing us the house took one look at my husband and beamed, "You'll love the upstairs. It's got really tall ceilings." *What about the downstairs?* I thought to myself. *I guess we'll have to stay upstairs.* Still, I was feeling a little bit hopeful. It turned out that the ceiling was maybe two feet higher than your average ceiling, which was not very high in those parts, and for that

she was charging an extra fifty thousand dollars! She could keep them.

Then came the clincher. We saw a one-family detached house, which should have been called a one-family detached bungalow, advertised for just $975,000. It was advertised as a "knock-down." No kidding. I might as well take my money and throw it into the trash. What were they thinking; three hundred, maybe four hundred thousand for a knock-down, but nearly a million dollars for something I was going to put a bulldozer through? He pointed to a beautiful house across the street on the same lot size and said this house could look like that. So why don't I take that one!

After a few weeks of this, I slowly became more open to the concept of moving to suburbia, and much to my husband's glee, I agreed to start meeting real estate agents in New Jersey. From that point on, we would spend nearly every Sunday for next six months viewing houses that made the houses in Queens look like miniatures and talking about lawns, parks, and decks where we could host large summer barbecues. I forgot for a moment what I would be missing— the conveniences of a supermarket on my street corner, a pizza store on every block, and a Main Street that bustled at 11:00 pm—and allowed myself to be gently pulled into the suburban dream.

2

How Come it Falls Apart the Second After You Move In?

I saw it and immediately realized that it was destined to be my home. It had the lawn, the park across the street, the synagogue around the corner, and the big backyard where I envisioned we'd spend long summer days lounging around with family. I'd purchase a hammock to string between the two perfectly situated trees, and there I'd relax (something I hadn't done or known how to do in years) and watch the star-lit sky. However, it took a little convincing to get my husband on the same page. We looked at what felt like another three hundred and fifteen other houses, but we always came back to the same house, and eventually it became ours. The house looked good from the outside, but it must have been held together with Scotch tape or Elmer's glue because as soon as we moved in, everything fell apart. I didn't want to appear ungrateful, but I secretly began to call our house "the money pit" after that wonderful movie that I was now able to relate to more and more with each passing day. It's about a house that looks mighty fine from the outside, but unravels like a spool of thread the second the owners moved in. Why didn't I get a sense of what was to come on my various walks through the house when we were finalizing our decision? I guess no one truly has any idea what they are getting themselves into when they buy a house, unless of course they build it from scratch, and I'm sure those people have plenty of headaches, too. Houses are like spouses in a way; you can only find out so much during the courtship. When you get married, you discover there was so much more to know. Maybe this is all for the best, because if every house (and spouse, for that matter) came with its own book of secrets, such as which faucets would remain forever leaky and which rooms would have drafts, which doors would mysteriously bang shut in the middle of the night and how thick the insulation between the walls really was, nobody would ever commit to buying a house. You'd have a world of renters and no buyers. Instead, you move in, and gradually the secrets of your house reveal themselves. Those problems that can be fixed, you fix, but some problems you just have to live with. I have come to the conclusion that we should all be able to live in a house for a week before buying it. It should be written into all real estate transactions. Before you formally go to contract, bring your pajamas and a warm blanket (or a fan if it's summer) and camp out in the house for a week. If after a week you can still deal with all the little things you've discovered, and hearing full conversations from the room adjacent to yours doesn't bother you, than the house should be yours.

I arrived home from work one day at my newly purchased house to find my kitchen was under water, and not just any water—hot water, *very* hot water was gushing out from under the sink, looking like an out-of-control fire hydrant. I quickly crawled under the sink with oven mitts and frantically tried to turn any knobs I could find in every which direction to keep Niagara Falls at bay. Apparently, my hot water dispenser had gotten locked in the on position and the pipe underneath was spouting boiling water all over my kitchen. I grabbed a dozen towels to sop up the impending storm and began calling every plumber within a thirty-mile radius, yelling into the phone, "I'm having an emergency at my house—boiling water is pouring out everywhere! Can you please come over and help me?" This yielded no fruit. I eventually called my handyman, who was most helpful, and he came right over and stopped the flood. He informed us that we would need a new hot water dispenser. I accepted this and paid him to do the work the next day.

No sooner had I turned over a small fortune to replace the hot water dispenser and gotten my kitchen pretty much cleaned up, than my dishwasher croaked. It started to sound like an earthquake was

moving through my house every time I tried to do a load of dishes, and eventually the motor gave out altogether, and the dishwasher was no more. The new dishwasher that was installed had a big handle that stuck out from the front (I seriously don't know who designs these things), which prevented my cutlery drawer from opening (the two were at a ninety degree angle from each other), so every time we needed a fork, we had to open the dishwasher. I guess there are worse things in life than eyeing your dirty dishes forty-seven times a day whenever you happen to want to grab a spoon or knife, but since I'm somewhat particular about these things, I called the store to have the dishwasher replaced with a flat-faced model. The poor delivery guy's truck broke down on the way to my house, and from the looks of the new dishwasher when it arrived at my house ten hours later, I think it must have rolled off the truck because it had a large dent across the front, and we had to send it back. By now I was ready to pull my hair out. It had been weeks since I had a working dishwasher in the house, and I was not loving my new role as the dishwasher. I kept on badgering the people at the appliance store, who by then had my phone number in their memory and were avoiding my calls, begging them to finally send the new model. I was starting to feel sorry for myself until the delivery man, who was returning for the third time to my house, informed me that he didn't even have a dishwasher in his house. Here I was sweating the small stuff, getting all excited about scrubbing a few dirty pots, while my delivery man was busy delivering and installing dishwashers all day long and he didn't have one himself. It made me stop for a moment and realize that I was getting bogged down by the minutiae of life and was not appreciating the bigger picture. At least I had a house, a warm bed, food in my fridge, heat in the winter … and one day, hopefully before I was ready to close up the house and retire to Florida, I'd have a dishwasher.

Eventually we got it all straightened out, and we had a new flat-faced dishwasher installed. We started to settle into our comfortable existence where everything was working fine ... for about fifteen whole minutes.

No sooner did we have a working dishwasher than my refrigerator decided to open every time someone walked by as if in greeting. Our handyman, who by this point was at my house every other day and was on speed dial, said all he needed to do was tilt the refrigerator back on its hind legs so that gravity could work to close the door, and the problem should be solved. I was excited at this seemingly quick (and cost-effective) fix until my grapes and tomatoes began rolling to the back of my fridge, and I had to fish out moldy tomatoes that had taken up refuge in the back of my fridge that I had forgotten I had ever purchased.

No sooner did my refrigerator get repaired than the knob broke off of my microwave. I endured one hundred calls to the manufacturer, and a few good hours getting routed around electronic phone systems, before I finally was able to speak to an actual person. They sent a repair man who had to replace what seemed like the entire insides of my microwave, all for a broken knob. Their view, according to the repair man, was once the microwave is installed, it's in for life, and they'd rather replace every part than have to take out the actual microwave and install a new one. Whatever works for them.

I found it amazing that I was keeping down a job with the repair schedule I was keeping track of. I felt it was time to add a special addendum to my daily prayers for my appliances and the general well-being of my house: "Please G-d, let all of my appliances function well today, let the plumbing in my house stay solvent, let no pipes burst, toilets overflow, water pressure drop down to a trickle when we're showering, heating system blow when its five degrees outside ...." It wasn't a joke. I was quickly discovering that my house needed my prayers just as much as my family and I did.

A few years later, when things got quiet for a time, my two-year-old decided he wanted to be the next Picasso and began creating works of modern art on my furniture and walls with any writing instrument he could get his hands on. I would walk around behind him with a Magic Eraser, the kind they advertise on television that gets out everything from ink to grease, but as fast as I erased, he seemed to scribble even faster. We'd have a competition; I'd erase the new designs he'd scribble on the back of my kitchen chairs, and by the time I looked up, the kitchen walls and a few of the cabinets were decorated as well. Every time I turned around, there was a new piece of "art" on the walls or furniture. We had to keep all pens, markers, crayons, and the like glued to the ceiling to keep his artistic ambitions at bay.

There came a point when I wished I knew how to fix things around the house myself instead of feeling so helpless and frustrated every time something broke. Unfortunately, Crazy Glue was my go-to product for fixing things. Whether it was a knob, a belt, a shoe, or a small appliance, I would take out my handy tube of Crazy Glue to see if I could fix it myself first. As you might guess, the larger problems didn't respond well to this fix. I began wondering why my college hadn't offered me the really important courses in life, such as Home Repairs 101, instead of classes like fencing, debate, and early American history, which I took instead. The only time debate class came in handy was when I debated with customer service over whether my refrigerator problems should be covered under the warranty I specifically purchased for repairs (they always tried to insist that whichever problems my appliance developed happened not to be included in the plan). I wished I knew how to do more around the house myself. What use was there in knowing when General Custer made his last stand if my custard wasn't standing anymore because my fridge was leaning over like the Tower of Pisa, or my oven croaked with all the food half-baked inside just before ten guests arrived for the weekend.

College should train you to be an adult, to know how to deal with the really important things in life, like corking a shower, unclogging a drain, and fixing a dryer. These should be mandatory courses required for graduation so that one doesn't break into a cold sweat every time something needs to be repaired and reach for a bottle of Valium to avoid an impending panic attack. Until that time, I guess we'll all have our handyman's phone number on speed dial and keep adding a special psalm for the appliances into our morning prayers.

3

Decorating Your Home

Suburbia was taking a whole lot more getting used to than I expected. I was trying to decorate my house during my newfound free time, before I began job hunting, and one day I decided to try to find a picture frame. (I had stopped working shortly after we moved in to get the house in order). It shouldn't have been complicated; I was looking for a simple sixteen-by-twenty-inch natural wood frame for a black and white baby picture of my son, the kind where everything is black and white except the blue ball he's holding. I was decorating his nursery and had found the perfect spot for it above his changing table, which was also finished in natural wood. I thought IKEA would be a good place to start, and so I packed my son into his car seat and set out on Route 4 toward the closest store. I saw a sign on the side of the road that read "IKEA Drive," and less than five seconds later there was an exit off the highway to IKEA; not in a half mile like most normal highways, but literally you blinked and you missed it, that's how close the exit was. The problem was I was still in the left lane. I missed the exit of course and had to go three miles on the wrong highway—the Garden State Parkway—before I could turn around and retrace my steps. That's New Jersey for you. You see a sign for an exit, and you'd better be in high gear because you've got to get off the highway immediately or you'll end up having to drive for a decade until you reach the next exit and can finally turn around. At times like these, I missed city driving, where there weren't so many rules in place. Or if there were, no one seemed to know them. If you're driving in one direction, and suddenly you see a store you like on the other side of the street, all you have to do is go to the corner, make a nice big U-turn, and vavoom, you are now on the other side of the street and can drop into your store. (Okay, I left out the fact that you may have to circle for an hour to look for parking, but that is a story for another day).

In New Jersey, say you are driving on Route 4 west and you see a store on the opposite side of the highway on Route 4 east that you want to check out. You can't just cross three lanes of traffic and pull right in; you may very likely have to drive another two miles and take one of those overpasses they've built to take you back on the highway in the reverse direction to get to your destination. It may end up taking you another five or ten minutes to get somewhere that was within arm's reach, but when you get there, you'll have miles and miles of parking, which some may say would make up for it.

At IKEA, I walked around for what seemed like an eternity, through a total of about fifteen different sections, each of which could have been its own store, to find my wooden picture frame. I finally got smart and decided to find a checkout counter and ask the salesperson where I could find the picture frames.

"Oh sure, it's all the way at the end of the third section to your right behind Marketplace."

"Sure" I said, but it was all Greek to me. I finally found the correct section, spotted my frame, and proceeded to drag it, with my baby carriage in tow, to the front of the store. They wanted to charge me for the plastic bag—some energy conservation program they had going on. Costco, I later learned, has a "no bag" policy, and you'll find ladies rushing out with three bags of bread in each hand and no bag in sight. I decided to forgo the fifty cents they were charging for the bag at IKEA and walked out to the parking lot holding my picture frame in one hand and pushing my baby stroller with the other, looking very much like I was doing a balancing act for the Big Apple circus.

Upon exiting the store, I realized immediately that I was in

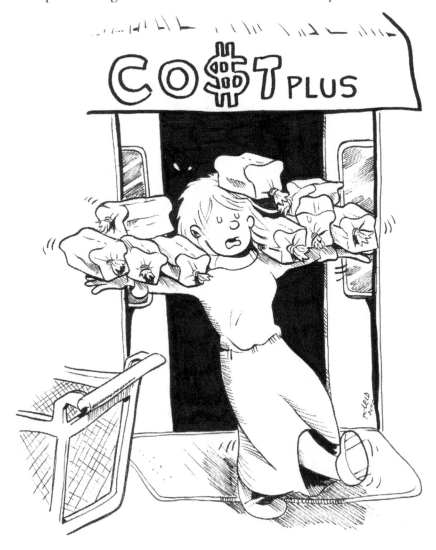

trouble. There were two gargantuan parking lots in front of me, and I could not remember where I had parked my car. How come this never happened to me in Queens? I was lucky if I only circled the block five times before snatching up a spot as someone was walking to their car dangling a ring of keys, so by then I'd remember where the spot was. But back at the IKEA parking lot, I was hopelessly lost. I began forlornly going up and down the rows of the parking lot, pressing my alarm clicker every fifty feet or so, hoping to locate my car. About half an hour later, my car came to life; it was in the back of the second garage. It took an hour and a half in total to get to the store, pick up my frame, and bring it home (something that would have taken me fifteen minutes in Queens because I could have just walked to the store from my apartment). By the time I got home, I was ready for a nap. Maybe tomorrow I'd try getting a broom.

This leisurely pace was really starting to get to me. It was dramatically different than the semi-manic pace I had gotten accustomed to while living in the city, and I was not sure if I liked it. It could certainly grow on me, I imagined, given enough time, but at that point it was making me lethargic and disoriented. I would just have to cut the list of things I needed to do each day into quarters and get used to the slower pace of life around here. But then, wasn't that what this whole suburbia thing was about—slowing the pace, catching your breath, smelling the roses, whiffing something besides smog and pollution. Hadn't we all moved here because we desperately needed to slow down, because the chaotic pace of city life was running us down and aging us by the minute, and we had gotten so caught up in all the things we had to do every minute of every day that we didn't really enjoy any of it? Here in suburbia, somehow it didn't seem as important to have a matching pair of shoes to each outfit or the latest CD, gadget, style, fad, and accessory that came on the market. People just didn't seem to care as much if you wore yesterday's style and didn't have tomorrow's hairdo. Actually, I had been spacing my hair appointments farther apart than ever before and making do with my clothes from a season or two ago, and so far, no one had arrested me. Instead, people were complementing me. I knew all of this cerebrally. I knew living here was probably best for me and my family. I knew that if we stayed in the 'burbs, my children would grow up calmer and hopefully with more inner peace than I had grown up with. I was pretty sure they wouldn't have that restless feeling that they always had to be on the move, that there was always one more thing to do and one more concert/play/show to attend. Tomorrow was just fine, and they'd never know the urgency of "Now! Now! Now!" the culture that defines city living.

I knew that the less competitive life out here in the suburb we had chosen would probably make them better, more content human beings in the long run and that one day they'd thank me, and I'd know I did right by them, but sometimes I still missed the noise and the energy of city life. I'd see my kids in the park, playing happily in the big, open, green fields when I would get home from work, and they seemed really happy. They didn't seem to miss anything—they had friends, they had space, they had fresh air to breathe, they still looked up when a fire truck passed and it excited them. They had a front yard *and* a backyard with a swing set and riding toys galore. How different their childhood experience would be than mine. Where I grew up on my crowded street in Brooklyn, there was someone living below me, on top of me, and on either side of me, and there was not a blade of grass in sight. If you wanted grass, you went to the park, and even there grass was sparse. We devised "grassless" games such as highligh, where you had a paddle attached to an elastic string with a rubber ball that you hit countless times. There was also jump rope, or footsie, or many other varied ball bouncing games that we'd play while singing some jingle until we dropped the ball and the next person got a turn. This is how I grew up, and somehow I didn't feel I lacked much.

If you wanted a playdate, you could open your window and check out who was outside because they were all right there, either in front of your house or in front of the house across the street. We didn't know about things like scheduling a playdate. Everyone who wanted to play was already outside. And it didn't matter the weather—winter, spring, summer, or fall—we just added a few layers or took off a few and played outdoors. Suburbia seemed so much more formal somehow, with all the arranging and all the planned playdates. I think a little spontaneity would be good for the kids here. You want to play with someone, you go downstairs and find out who is there, or you just walked over to whoever's house you want to play with and knock on the door. Growing up, nobody thought you were strange or intruding if you just showed up. Here, my sons have a busier social calendar than I do, and it takes quite a bit of energy to arrange all their "dates."

There is a lot to be said about the pros and cons of city life versus suburbia, but I believe we each try to take all the factors into account and do what's best for ourselves and our families. One thing I can say is that for most of us, the place where we grew up always feels like home. Many kids who grew up in the suburbs of New Jersey get married, live in the city for a few years, and bring their families right back here. They have fond memories of growing up with rabbits, chipmunks, and squirrels; of birds flying all about; and of big houses and more relaxed mothers—and they want the same for their children. And I gather the same can be said for kids who grew up in the cities (but somehow this seems less common). Overall, most adults feel most at home in a place with similar qualities and energy levels as the place they grew up, and I suspect a part of us always wants to return there.

4

Antiquing

Yesterday I went antiquing. Living in suburbia, it is just something you do. I was in the process of furnishing my house, so on the advice of my decorator, we took a trip to the antique district in Central New Jersey. I tell you, you could take all of my old junk, put it in a store, call it "antique," and someone else could be paying me for it. I have never seen such a scam. They're selling all the contents of my grandmother's apartment—which makes me depressed every time I look at them because they are so old—call them antiques so they're suddenly incredibly valuable, and I'm supposed to pay good money for them. The shop looked like a converted barn and smelled like a nursing home. It was damp and cold. They couldn't afford heating after selling all these treasures? Or maybe they were trying to contribute to the "antique" mood circa the 1850s, before modern heating was invented. Whatever their intentions, I was freezing in there and looking for the nearest exit.

My husband hates antiques. He tried to straighten me out when I started decorating our house: "No antiques!" he said. He hates old things. They depress him (and make him feel mortal, I guess!), but I decided I'd at least take a look and see what everyone else was so excited about. However, after looking at the rows and rows of green-and-orange-flowered furniture, hundreds of candelabras that looked like they were robbed from the haunted house in Disney World, cobwebs and all, and zillions of dishes, I turned to my forlorn decorator and said, "Sorry, no antiques." My husband likes young, modern, hip things that remind him of youth, life, hope, and the future, not jewelry that my great-grandmother would have rejected. I bid the whole smelly ship good-bye and looked longingly at the Ethan Allen down the road.

Decorating my house had become my occupation, as I didn't get an actual job for many months. I found a decorator who looked the part and hired her pretty much on the spot. I've always imagined it must be quite difficult to be a decorator. You can never let your hair down, even when you are taking out your garbage. You have to make sure you look all made up and are wearing your heels and a stylish outfit, lest your neighbors or a potential client see you running out the door with a rag on your head and the latest find from the bottom of your closet and decide that if that's how *you* look, that's how *their* house will look after you're done with it. Every interior decorator I've ever came across has been a walking advertisement for her job. She (yes, it usually is a she) is impeccably dressed from head to toe with not a hair out of place, wearing high heels everywhere, even on the beach or taking out the garbage, and looking like she just stepped out of the pages of a fashion magazine. They all seem to have coordinating boots, jackets, and purses that are always at the height of fashion. You take one look at them and want to hire them as your personal clothing shopper as well as your interior decorator. I met mine at a lecture. I was shopping around for interior decorators and got a few names, and then a friend of mine pointed her out to me at a lecture and the match was made. We had a lot of fun shopping together, first for furniture, rugs, tables, and the like, and then, after spending that much time together and learning everything else about each other, we became great friends and went shopping for clothes, shoes, and accessories for ourselves and the kids.

An interior decorator is like a hairdresser, in that you eventually spill your guts to both of them. There aren't many other people, beside your therapist if you have one, who you will spend that much time with and who will get such an up close and personal look at your life and finances. She will learn what your approximate household worth is, as there will be times you will have to say no to certain exquisite things she points out that are simply above your budget. She will learn how you and your spouse interact and problem solve, i.e. Do you have the kind of marriage where your husband makes the money, gives you carte blanche over running the house, and lets you buy whatever you want within his means? Does he want no part of running or furnishing the house, trusts your decisions implicitly, and just wants to see the finished product, or do you have the type of marriage where every rug, lamp, and picture frame must be run by him first before purchasing it? This type of man has an opinion about everything and wants a say in everything, from what colors you pick for the walls to what knickknacks you pick for the coffee table. Your decorator will learn how you and your husband solve disputes, as in cases where you fall in love with a chair that he thinks is hideous, and you go into negotiating/begging mode trying to convince him how lovely it would look in your living room. And then come the inevitable money disagreements, where you get all excited over all the beautiful things your decorator has chosen with you and are ready to buy them all, but your husband begins to panic and reminds you that he has not come into a giant inheritance as of yet, and you have to curtail your enthusiasm and restrain yourself for the time being. He tells you to just pick a few pieces you like now and save the rest to purchase at a later time. That's when many women go into the negotiating phase—which items should they get now and which should they save for later? Or maybe they decide to return to work, or increase their work hours, so they can afford all the wonderful things they've chosen.

It's no wonder that after working so closely with my decorator for over six months, she became my closest friend. I had just moved into the neighborhood and meeting new people was going slower than I would have liked. She was always upbeat, cheery, and optimistic and dressed to the nines—plus she knew all the great cafés and interesting hot spots in town—so we became great friends. There's a Jewish proverb that goes "Thou shall purchase for thyself a friend." I guess I did!

The problem was what happened when I finished decorating my house and still wanted her as my friend. I wondered if I still had to pay her if we went for coffee together and she mentioned something about fashion or furniture. *Was that considered work or play?* I wondered. At what point did my professional relationship with her end and my friendship with her start? I really wanted her as a friend, especially since I could bypass all the initial awkwardness involved in getting to know someone and sharing personal details with them. She knew all of that already, and we could just move on to the comfortable friendship stage. The day we went antiquing was one of those confusing days in our relationship. We both had babies the same age and decided to picnic together in a quaint, waterside town about a forty-five minute drive from where we lived. It was going to be a fun, relaxing day and our kids could play together and give us some time to relax. I packed some sandwiches, and we picked up some drinks and snacks along the way. We set out our blankets and lunches by the water and had a wonderful time as our kids chased each other around the grassy area alongside the lake. We then put them in their strollers and went walking around the town and discovered some really cool antique shops. We started going in, as she mentioned she was a big antique fan, and game for almost anything, I trailed along. I was slightly concerned about my fifteen-month-old getting his hands on some very valuable antique dishes and using them as Frisbees, but I held on to him as best as I could and followed close behind. As I mentioned previously, I'm not a big fan of antiques, but I was curious about what all the hoopla was about, and shopping with someone who has incredible taste for anything, even cereal brands, can be fun.

In our third or fourth store (this one wasn't an actual antique store but a regular furniture store) she pointed out a rug that I thought was absolutely magnificent and would be the perfect addition to my living room. We had been looking for weeks for a rug, and finally we found the perfect one. The question then became, do I pay her for the time in the store? The hour? The day? I was clueless and wondered if our day picnicking would go into the expense column or friendship column. In the end I didn't get the rug. Phew! But I tell you, the relationship did get confusing at times. Thankfully, I eventually finished decorating my house (although an interior decorator might say that you're never truly finished, you can always add a pillow here, or a frame there, but my husband informed me that the decorating was definitely finished), and we went on to be great friends. We never went antiquing again.

5

Cars, Cars, and More Cars

When I agreed to move to suburbia with my spouse, I knew there would be some transition involved, but by far the most difficult thing about suburbia to adjust to was not seeing anyone on the streets during the day except for the mailman and UPS delivery persons, and if I was lucky, an occasional nanny pushing a stroller. When I first arrived here, this drove me batty. *Where are all the people?* I wondered. Even if I wondered aloud, there was no one around to hear me and look at me funny for conversing with myself. I even composed a ditty in my spare time:

Oh where, oh where have the people gone,
Oh where, oh where can they be?
If anyone finds some people I say, please return them to me.

There seemed to be lots of houses and thousands of cars, especially minivans, so I knew there had to be people, but I just didn't seem to be fortunate enough to find any of them. Being a social creature who was happiest walking down a busy avenue in the city surrounded by throngs of people going about their daily routines, I found this especially difficult to adjust to. I would take a walk with my baby in the stroller each morning, and I would be the only one walking outside for miles and miles. I'd see squirrels, birds, rabbits, cars, and rows of pretty houses, but not a soul. I might as well have been living on Saturn. I longed for people to come out of their big, comfortable houses; I'd be happy if they even just peeked out the window so I could be sure there were indeed other human beings inhabiting this part of the planet with me. I found myself engaging in lengthy conversations with delivery men, mailmen, and anyone else I could find on the street that would stop and chat because I so badly needed the human interaction.

I soon discovered that the reason I couldn't find any people on the street was because there weren't any. They were all in their cars. If you wanted to see people you just had to look into car windows; that is, if you can catch them while they were stopping for a red light or stop sign because in suburbia, I quickly discovered, nobody believes in walking. They use their cars for everything. Your kid has a playdate around the corner and needs to be picked up, you hop in the car. You're in middle of baking and you run out of sugar, you drop everything and hop in your car. You get the sniffles and need a box of tissues, you jump in the car. People would pass me in their minivans, and I longed for them to stick their heads out the window and chat. (The minivan, I found out, is another suburban must-have. First, you need the house, the big lawn, and the kids, and then you had to have the perfect minivan parked in the driveway.) It made me wonder, *Whatever happened to good, old-fashioned fresh air and a good walk?* I guess the gyms and treadmills made this sentiment a thing of the past. I was starting to feel like Forrest Gump with all the walking I was doing, but instead of "Run, Forrest, run," it was "Walk, Sharon, walk." Maybe if I walked enough, this walking thing would catch on. *I could start a trend*, I thought. *Walking in suburbia … what a novel concept … leave your stuffy cars at home and come and enjoy the great outdoors.* I'd start a movement to bring people out of their big houses and cars and onto the streets so I could fill my desperate need to see other human beings.

Even if you wanted exercise, you still got in your car—to drive to the gym, that is. Nobody walks. They don't even know what that is. The most they will do is drive their cars to the gym or mall and do their "laps" or exercise there by walking from one side of the mall to the other. I'm not kidding. A friend called me up shortly

after we moved in and asked if I'd like to go with her to the mall, not to shop, but to exercise. She would walk from one side of the mall to the other for about an hour and call that her exercise. (The mall, I later found out, is the main street of suburbia. Everyone eventually ends up at the mall. If there is one thing suburbia has plenty of, it's malls—hundreds of them in all shapes and sizes, selling everything your heart desires so you end up shopping until you drop. I learned that if I wanted to see people, I would have to follow them to the mall, and that's where I eventually found all my neighbors.)

Another individual I met shortly after moving in was getting into her car one day. I asked her where she was going. She informed me that she drives three miles every day to a park to do her daily exercise; she walks around the track. She said she's embarrassed for anyone to see her here because she doesn't feel good about her physique, so she drives three miles a day to a park in another town where she won't be seen. I just couldn't get used to the idea of having to get into a car to do just about everything.

After a while I realized if I can't beat 'em, I should join 'em, so after walking the streets for months and not succeeding in swaying anyone to follow behind, I got into my car and started following the hoards to find out where they were going. Maybe I was missing something. Maybe I could find out where everyone was so busy driving to with such intense determination, and I could join them. I'd go to all the malls and all the popular suburban hot spots such as Target, Trader Joe's, Costco, and Best Buy and try to seek out my fellow suburbanites. I even drove five miles one day to get a bag of chocolate chips. Okay, they weren't just any chocolate chips. They were Trader Joe's super chocolaty chocolate chips, but nevertheless, I was pretty shocked at my determination to go out of my way for these chocolate chips. Now that I wasn't working, and I could dedicate a whole afternoon to baking chocolate chip cookies (so I can bribe my parents to come visit me out here), I was doing things like traveling half an hour to get the ideal chocolate chips for my cookies. That day I looked into the car mirror and said, "Sharon, you just may be turning into a suburbanista."

6

Back to Dating

Today I had my first coffee date. I guess that's what you do in suburbia: playdates, library dates, and coffee dates. If you want to see other members of the human race, you can't just open your front door, as I had gotten used to doing in the past. You have to schedule a "date." I have to tell you, I was craving some spontaneity—if your kid is getting bored, just bring 'em over; we have plenty of toys at my house. If you want to see a friendly face, holler about the injustices of life, complain about your nanny, or see another Homo sapien, just knock on my door, I won't bite. I'll just be happy to see you and even invite you in for coffee (that you don't have to pay three bucks for). I tend to fly by the seat of my pants, and all this scheduling was driving me a little batty. I have to admit, I found it quite unnerving at first. Why did everything have to be a "date?" I thought I was happily done with that when I wed my husband. Did that mean I had to suffer the rejection all over again? And what about my kids? If they and their "dates" didn't hit it off, would I get a call from a disgruntled parent saying, "Nice kid, but we don't think he's for us?" This I knew I could live without.

Overall, the higher level of formality that existed here, coupled with not working and having much too much free time on my hands, was more change than I had bargained for. My daily schedule went from jam-packed to nearly empty in one day. Okay, not completely empty, but compared to what I was used to before the move, I had plenty of unfilled time. The first week I moved in I was busy with the house. The second week I was schlepping things home from Brooklyn and still busy with the house. (Okay, I'm originally from Brooklyn, and Brooklyn gals will do that—wherever we move, we'll always come back to the mother ship to do our shopping.) By the third week I was bored and no longer busy with the house. Not that there weren't things to do; I just got bored of comparing tile patterns for my bathroom that still needed to be finished and pricing dinette sets and decided to face up to life in suburbia. There were three things I noticed right away.

A. I was spending an inordinate amount of time in supermarkets (which is another place, I soon discovered, where you can meet people).

B. I'd buy about two items at the supermarket on each trip, ensuring that I'd have to go back again later that day or tomorrow for something else.

C. I was bored.

The prospect of going back to work was looking more appealing by the minute.

However, at least people here were nice. The Verizon guy waited twenty minutes one day at my house while I was picking up "a few things" at the supermarket so he could show me how to work all the electrical gadgets in the house that we had accumulated. That gave me some hope that maybe I'd adjust to this place one day—just maybe!

7

Mommy & Me

It's funny how the high school cliques you hoped to never see again follow you through life. You think you're finished with them the day you graduate, throwing your hat up in the air with glee, and thinking to yourself, *I will never be snubbed by another snotty girl—*ever*! I will never walk over to a lunch table and reach for the last seat and have someone smile at me all too politely while possessively putting their hands over the back of the chair and say, 'It's taken.'*

I will never have to fret if my clothes were sporting the right designer labels or if they are year of two out of date, or who I'm going to sit next to at a school trip because in real life, I imagined, everyone would be nice and eager to sit near me. But I discovered as I move gracefully into adulthood that the cliques just move along with you. They may have one or two more laugh lines around their mouths and one or two more bags under their eyes, but they are still the cool girls who stand off to the side of the room whose whole purpose seems to be to make you feel like you have grown a huge watermelon out of your head. This time, however, it's their kids who are wearing the designer labels and getting all the playdates, while yours are standing sheepishly glued to your skirt, wearing a plaid shirt two sizes too small with one button closed and an Elmo sweat suit underneath (at least that was in style, I think) that they insisted on wearing that day.

I learned this lesson early on as I took my son to a Mommy & Me class at the local Gymboree and saw a group of these "cool" women congregating off to the side, whispering to each other as if they were sharing the most exciting news in the world. I planted myself not too close so they didn't think I was eavesdropping (which I was), and not too far away so I couldn't hear what they were saying and placed a very disinterested look on my face as I tried painfully to catch a word or two of their lively chatter. These "cool" people have this incredible way of always sounding like they are in the midst of planning the most incredible event on earth, which from the little bits and pieces you catch always seems to be something that would be great fun and you'd do anything to be there. This time they were talking about children's clothing (I didn't know that children's clothing could generate such excitement, but I listened intently). Thinking that I was missing something extraordinary in the children's clothing world, I mustered up the courage to ask one of them, "Where is the sale going on?" They looked at me, and said in unison, "It's private." There I was again, reduced to my ninth grade insecurities, wondering how I could obtain an entrance pass to this coveted private label designer children's clothing sale, or were my kids destined to wear whatever was on the sale rack at Target last season.

I guess it's just something you have to eventually come to accept. The cliques never go away. They change size and shape and put on a few pounds and lose a few hairs but they're always there. I wonder if in the nursing home they all sit at the same table as well and compare grandchildren stories ….

"Hey Sadie, did you hear what my Joshua did?"

"No, but after you tell me, I just have to tell you what my Samantha did."

"He's only two years old, and he's been hanging out a lot in the park now that the weather is getting nicer. He went over to a group of girls, all about his age that he plays with, and said, "Hi ladies."

"If you think that's funny, Samantha just learned how to … " and so on.

As for the Gymboree class itself, my son had no interest in it at all. He would have been much more excited had I given him my car keys and let him sit in the driver's seat for an hour so he could turn on all the lights and press all the buttons. Actually, that's exactly what happened. My son's absolute favorite activity is "driving" my car. There is no toy, gadget, device, or electronic equipment in the world that excites him as much as pretending to drive (or if I'd allow him to, actually driving) my car. So the first day we get to Gymboree, my son sang, danced, ran around, played bubbles and jumped off big inflatable toys, all of which I thought should be pretty exciting for a two-year-old, but the most exciting part by far was when we left the class and he turned to me and said, "Vroom, vroom, Mommy's car." I knew exactly what he meant; he wanted to drive my car. And since I had an hour or two to spare, as I had returned to work at this point at a reduced work schedule so I could spend more quality time with him (though I was having second thoughts about this), I naively acquiesced. I opened the door, gave him my keys, and he proceeded to jump into the driver's seat. For the next hour he tried to get my keys into the ignition, and proceeded to turn every light on and off, blow the horn, turn on the emergency brake lights, and did everything else he could possibly think of. It was all fun for him, but after one hour of this, my car didn't start and I had to call AAA to get a jump. What a fun morning that was.

The next week I got smarter and actually brought jumper cables with me, so that when the same thing happened and my car wouldn't start, I got a jump from one of the ladies coming out of the next Gymboree class. What I've noticed about my kids is that no matter what toys or gadgets I bought them, they tended to be far more enthralled with the real thing. Who wants a little purple and yellow plastic car when you can have the real thing? And who wants a silly kitchen set with little plastic cutlery when you can bang around Mommy's much more exciting and noisy pots and pans?

As for me, whenever I get bored, I go out and buy my son a toy (having him is a very convenient excuse for buying myself toys). What actually happens is that we as adults buy the toys for ourselves. Our kids, after all, get bored of them after 2.3 seconds and go on to play with the neighbor's toys, which for some reason are always much more interesting than their own, and we end up playing with our kids' toys. I love my kids' toys. They should just stop all the false advertising and correctly state, "Here is our brand-new Fisher Price animal circus, geared for adults ages eighteen to one hundred," because your kids will end up getting bored with it before it even gets out of the box, and you will be chasing them around with the adorable circus people that you are having so much fun with, trying to balance all six of them on your head without toppling them over, all while riding a unicycle, while your three-year-old is out in the garage actually trying to mount your real bicycle.

8

Nannies for Hire

"Anita, I'm looking for Anita," I screamed at three random women standing at a bus stop near my house. I had arranged to pick up the nanny candidate that I was supposed to interview at ten thirty today at a nearby bus stop, and I was trying desperately to locate her. Her original interview had been scheduled for yesterday, but she got lost on the way to my house. She called me while wandering around Grand Central Station (she was supposed to be at the George Washington Bridge), and we rescheduled for today. I tried to make it as easy as possible for her to get to me by agreeing to pick her up from the bus stop so that she doesn't have to chance getting lost as she's walking to my house. I truly felt like I lived in the sticks. No one seemed to be able to find my house. There must be a whole stream of nannies wandering around Northern New Jersey holding pathetic-looking, scrunched up pieces of paper with my home address in their hand, still trying their very hardest to get to my house for their interviews. The truth is, I'd probably get lost too if I were them. New Jersey can be a confusing mess. There's Ridgewood and Ringwood (what about ringworm?) and Hohokus and Hackensack. If you're not confused enough, there's Edgewater and Riveredge and Northvale and Montvale, and let's not forget the Oranges. We've got East, West, and South Orange to add to the confusion. Who made up these names, anyway? Sometimes I feel like every two blocks is another town, and each person says their town name, like "Hi, I'm from Lodi," or "Hi, I'm from "North Bergen" like it's the most important place on earth and I should know and understand the subtle cultural identity and flavor of their city as if it's vastly different than the town three blocks away. Well, I don't. I think it would have been a lot easier had they just called the whole thing New Jersey and given each town numbers. I live in town 1; she lives in town 47 … and so on. One mayor, one board—keep the whole thing really easy. I used to say that any nanny who can find her way to my house is hired; now I say if they have a pulse, then they're hired. I would set up six interviews, every hour on the hour for six hours and not be terribly concerned that they'd bump into each other on the way in or out of my house, or worse yet, all show up at the same time. (Wouldn't that be fun? A group interview.) This was because out of the six interviews I'd set up, only about two or three would show up.

The nanny I was to meet on this day, if I ever found her and decided to hire her, would be the seventh nanny I'd hired that year. I was seriously ready to pull my hair out, and my poor kids didn't know what had hit them. Every other Monday, a new lady showed up at my front door to take care of them. I was almost ready to throw the towel in on the whole career thing. Maybe this was a sign that I had chosen the wrong path in life and should reconsider the whole stay-at-home-mom thing. As it was, I was feeling so guilty about my decision to go back to work (especially when my son mashed his nose against the window each morning as I was going on interviews, looking puppy-dog sad), and this nanny chaos with him having to get used to a new one every week or so wasn't helping matters at all. I came home from work one day shortly after being hired at my job.

I was up to nanny # 6, and I had decided to pay her a "surprise" visit in middle of the day and see how she was managing. It was about twelve in the afternoon, and my three-month-old was sitting in front of the television and my eighteen-month-old was yelling from his crib. The nanny was taking a shower. I knew I was in trouble when I discussed this with my mother-in-law, who said, "Trust your gut." This was the nanny equivalent of having a watermelon thrown at my gut. I was so desperate to have the help at home so I could continue my work schedule and finish the week that I let her stay until Friday and popped in on her every day and called about every five minutes to see how she was doing. In a complete state of panic, I called three nanny agencies and had forty women from every country in the Caribbean call me looking for a job, all the while trying to get some work done myself.

There was sixty-three-year-old Sandra, who, according to her reference was, despite her advanced age, "healthier than me or you." She wanted over five hundred dollars a week to watch my kids, but she wouldn't lift a finger in my house; no wonder she's healthier than me or you. There was Maggie, who kept calling every five minutes and whining into the phone that her current boss was only paying her three hundred dollars a week and she was responsible for four kids. She kept on telling me how she was looking for more money. Just listening to her groan on the phone for two minutes was more than I could bear. I couldn't imagine sharing a roof with her.

I don't know if it was me or the nannies that I chose to hire, but I couldn't get one to stay. I started to worry that maybe it was me, maybe I was a nanny slave driver. I expected too much from them and then wondered why I was on my seventh nanny in one year. Maybe I was just unrealistic about my expectations. *It's like dating*, I thought to myself, *sometimes you just have to lower your expectations.* Expecting someone to take care of a three-month-old and an eighteen-month-old and still find time to do the laundry, make the beds, clean the kitchen ... and the floors ... and the bathrooms ... all in the two hour span that the babies nap— And I almost forgot, help me prepare dinner—may be asking a little too much. I couldn't do all of that myself; I started to realize it was crazy for me to ask someone else to do it all for me.

I guess times were difficult, because I had so many nannies calling me for the position, I began getting thoroughly confused. I set up my interviews and began the process once again:

"So your name is Julia, right?"

"No, it's Maria."

"Oh, I'm so sorry Maria. You have an eleven-year-old son, I hear."

"No, I have a four-year-old daughter," she said, looking at me rather suspiciously. I had them coming in every hour from ten in the morning to four in the afternoon. Nanny #1 and nanny #2 successfully made it to my neighborhood (they deserve a medal—I'm not kidding), but they couldn't find their way to my house. My husband went to collect them from various bus stops when they got tired of wandering around my neighborhood and called me in frustration. Nanny #3 got mixed up between the George Washington Bridge (where she was headed) and Grand Central Station (where she ended up). She spent two hours milling around there before she got fed up and went home. Nanny #4, 5, and 6 never showed up.

I was getting desperate ....

Nanny #3 had quite an encouraging voice on the phone ("Everything was beautiful" according to her), so I decided to let her try to find her way again the following day. She did, and I hired her on the spot. I liked very much how she handled the whole ordeal of getting lost without completely losing her cool (as I probably would have), and I thought this was probably a good sign that she could handle the job. She started right away, and things finally looked like they would return to some semblance of normalcy after weeks of doing the nanny shuffle. The beginning with Lisa was a little tough, as for the first few weeks I kept on mistakenly calling her by the name of our previous nanny. My poor kids were completely frazzled and getting more cranky and clingy by the minute. Rule #1 in the nanny world: you've got to keep your nanny's name straight.

I thought I had it bad, but when I started to share my personal nanny horror stories with other people, I got reports that made my stories look tame. When my friend's daughter was seven years old, she came home from work to find her daughter immersed in a long discussion with the nanny about pregnancy—specifically, whether or not the nanny should keep her baby. My friend had no idea her nanny was pregnant, and she certainly did not want her seven-year-old making decisions about terminating pregnancies. The nanny confided to my friend that as she had already had a number of abortions and ultimately wanted to have a child, she decided to keep this one and was soon on her way. Another friend confided in me that her nanny had doctor's appointments every week. "She had such major medical problems (or she was very creative and made them up) that we hardly saw her … and then one day she didn't show up at all," leaving this poor lady in a lurch with a job she needed to leave for one morning and three children clinging to her legs. It seems like anyone you speak to who has had a nanny has a story to tell.

Still another woman I know had a nanny who offered to start coming early one day a week to clean the house, which my friend gladly agreed to. The only problem was the woman was somewhat elderly and had arthritis, a bad back, and was going blind from diabetes. The woman's house hadn't been cleaned in months, but she felt so bad letting go of this woman who had been with the family for six years that she kept her on and let her house go to shambles.

At times, I felt bad about leaving my children with nannies. The stay-at-home moms who are your friends will make you feel guilty for leaving your kids with random strangers while you're at work.

You'll wonder if you're making the right choices in life and if you'll have any deep-seated regrets later on. You hope that you won't be working this through with your kids in therapy years later when they feel they didn't get enough of your time or attention. It's all about "quality" time you tell yourself as you busily get down on all fours the second you walk through the door from work, throw off your coat, hat, and shoes, ask the nanny to throw some leftovers in the oven, and start zooming your son's Thomas trains all around the playroom in the hopes of making up for your absence all day. I really do try to give it my all when I get home, two hours of intense on-the-floor playing until their bedtime. The truth is that if I did stay home with them, I'd have to drop the energy a notch or two or I'd totally wear myself out and need a 9:30 am nap with my kids. I would have to just learn to relax with them and let them do their own thing without hyper-managing every second of our time together by creating circuses and plays for them and giving them airplane and "horsy" rides around the room. A stay-at-home mom I know says she just lets the kids play by themselves most of the day in the den, and she'll be busy at the computer nearby or taking care of some much needed household stuff.

Lately, my eighteen-month-old, who has been spending an inordinate amount of time in front of the television, will hand me the remote and say "Dee dee, Dee dee" (his way of saying TV) the second I walk through the door, signaling that he wants to watch with me. I think to myself, *how sad that he's not interested in my floor acrobatics and doesn't want to engage in my imaginative floor play but would rather sit next to me and watch 'Dee dee.'*

Sometimes it's your kids who guilt you about leaving them. My older son began having major temper tantrums when I'd leave for work in the morning, which made me feel terrible and abusive. I figured out how to get him engaged in an activity or toy so he was reasonably happy, and I'd give him this whole speech, "Tracy (or whoever was there that Monday) is going to take really good care of you today, and you're going to have a great time." In time he usually calmed down, and I was able to leave feeling a little less guilty. I also learned that if they see that you have a good rapport with the nanny (and it's really worth taking the time and making the effort to develop that rapport), your kids will feel more comfortable with the nanny and not be as devastated when you leave.

9

Costco-mania

I love Costco. I love the manic feeling I get when I walk in. I love the quick rush of energy that hits me when I enter the parking lot. I even love the frenzy of trying to find a parking space. My pulse quickens as I try to maneuver into the last parking spot before the five other people eyeing it from their cars. It is, after all, the only place in suburbia that reminds me of home. It is the only place that brings me back to the streets of Brooklyn before the Sabbath, or the week before Passover as everyone rushes around frantically getting their cases of potatoes, eggs, and oranges into their cars as if the grocery stores are permanently shutting down and don't reopen an hour after the holiday ends so one can restock. You see, I'd been trying for months to find a place in suburbia where I could feel truly alive, and for me, a born and bred city girl, that means frenzy, hustle and bustle, long lines, big sales with people lugging out half the store, and yes, even fighting for parking spaces.

The magic all began on November 4, 2007, when I received my first Costco membership and finally discovered where all of suburbia hangs out on cold Sunday mornings. I was thoroughly awed by the energy of the place, that and the fact that there were people who bought a bushel of Romaine lettuce large enough to feed a herd of cows and a case of granola bars that could satisfy a football team as if there was nothing to it. How do these people consume so much food? I wondered to myself. I started out slowly and gingerly packed up my gigantic wagon (they make their wagons absolutely huge so you feel absolutely pathetic buying only a few things) with maybe three to four items—bread, some tissues, and cups—as I watched everyone else cart away half the store. My favorite part was all the free food they were offering. I feasted on free David's cookies and chocolate pies, nuts and dried fruit until I almost puked. You can come in hungry and poof: it's lunch time. There are crackers and dips, chicken stews, fried fish, and a brand-new super brownie on the market in three new flavors —and they'll let you try all three. I've heard people literally come in on Sunday expecting to get a meal.

I got conned into buying twelve muffins that come in this lovely variety pack. I might as well have stuck a whole new wardrobe into the cart with them because I may need the next size or two after eating those mammoth-sized muffins that looked like they were on steroids. The city types are preoccupied with dieting, but not so in this corner of the world. Here everything is bought in bulk: huge containers, cases, family packs. Just looking at it all you felt your waist line growing. You get caught up in all the fun, and the excitement is contagious. You go in for onions and come out with a swing set. I discovered this amazing bread and went back for a few more loaves because according to the bag it "freezes well." I then discovered that I didn't have room in my freezer for all the extra loaves, so I quickly called up my neighborhood appliance store and had them send over a brand-new freezer. I was really a suburbanite now, new freezer and all, ready with an apple pie and a banana loaf to defrost should we ever have visitors. I was really on a roll and getting more caught up in the frenzy by the minute. I must have saved a fortune because I ended up with more things in my cart than you could consume in a decade. Everyone else seemed to be buying as much as me or more. The guy behind me on line must have owned a café because he bought four gallons of milk, three cases of three hundred and twelve tea bags, and five barrel-sized containers of coffee.

As much as I loved Costco, I didn't get the "no bag" thing. You're forced to stuff pineapples, bananas, melons, and oranges into your car like a crazed suburban lady and just hope when you get home you don't have a compote in your trunk.

Nowadays, I eagerly wait every month for my Costco wholesale coupon book to arrive in the mail. It usually has something like "$900 in savings inside" splashed across the top in big, bold lettering. Try as I may, I cannot figure out how many boxes of Kirkland baby wipes (the only thing I truly need in the entire coupon book) I'd have to buy at three dollars off to reach my $900 in savings.

At the end of the day, the place is fun and one of the few stores open in my area on a Sunday where for some reason, because of some political decision I'll never understand, most stores except supermarkets are closed on Sundays. Costco is allowed to be open, but they cordon off many of the aisles filled with things you are not allowed to buy, i.e. clothing, electronics, etc., so as not to have an unfair edge over the other stores that have to be closed on Sunday that sell these items. Either way, it's a great place to spend a few hours. I arrived one Sunday morning with my toddler, my newborn, and my spouse. We planted ourselves there for the whole morning. My husband perused the toys and children's books with my older son and I purchased a water bottle and sat myself on a comfortable lounger and fed my baby. Then after we were each done, we brought Kirkland frozen yogurt, available for sale in individual portions at the cafeteria, and sat down on the picnic tables and had a little feast.

Costco is the kind of store that once you get used to their products, you become an addict. There are just some things they do better, like their fruit, for example. Their fruit is so big that it's almost biblical. I always have to have a bag or two in the freezer of their delicious Kirkland individually-packaged frozen salmon and their cheesecakes and chocolate chip cookies, which are absolutely scrumptious. I found that after living in suburbia for a while, there are a few stores where I have become a regular shopper because there are certain products they each do better than the others. Take for example Trader Joe's chocolate chips, creamy tomato soup, and braided mozzarella sticks, or the large boxes of *Life* cereal from Target, or the prepared fish from ShopRite. I now have to go to four different stores, however, to do my shopping (I'm sounding like a real suburbanite, aren't I?). The truth is that after living here for three years, I've come a really long way and I'm actually getting used to this place. Okay, I'll admit, I even like it. It will never be Brooklyn, but I'm not sure now if I ever want it to be. I will always miss my parents and family who I see much less of now that I've moved away, but I'm starting to get my bearings around here, and I've even developed a certain fondness for suburban life.

10

The Making of a Deckel

"What, you don't know what a deckel is?" My aunt said to me accusingly, as if not knowing this made me a complete misfit in the domestic department. I responded somewhat sheepishly, "No, actually I don't. What is it?"

She proceeded to explain to me that a deckel is a type of meat that is used to make pot roasts and the like, and that every good woman running any sort of respectable household had to know how to make a good deckel. I was determined to quickly remove any blemishes from my culinary reputation and immediately find out what exactly a deckel was. I was determined to make a deckel so delicious that it could take home the "Deckel of the Year" award. I would become expert of the deckel and be able to whip up a fabulous one the next time my aunt came by for a dinner or party.

The problem was, ashamed as I was to admit it, my family ate mostly chicken. Meats, roasts, briskets, London broils—they all scared me. I get lost in the world of cuts and animal anatomy. I would usually stay away from them because I was afraid of ruining a perfectly good piece of meat (and usually pretty pricey, too) by not having the faintest clue what I was doing. I would cook the poor roast 'till it was all black and shriveled, and then we'd all be chomping away furiously trying to digest the piece of rubber. People would tell me, "You need to buy a meat thermometer," so I went out and bought one, but none of us could agree how exactly we liked our meat. My husband liked his medium-rare, I liked mine medium-well, so this didn't solve our problems. A deckel, it seemed, could be cooked in tons of liquid, just like a pot roast, for many hours and therefore was pretty hard to botch up, so I proceeded to the meat section of my local supermarket to find myself a deckel. I was really excited when I spotted my deckel and proceeded to buy the rest of the ingredients I needed for the recipe and took them to the cash register. This was an easy one: just two onions thinly sliced, whole berry cranberry sauce, and onion soup mix all poured on the deckle and cooked together for two-and-a-half hours at 325 degrees in a covered baking dish—even I could handle this recipe.

When I got home I washed my deckel, poured on the ingredients, and let it bake for the allotted time. The results were amazing, and I felt closer than ever to regaining my position as a proper suburban housewife (which I actually wasn't, as by then I had been working almost full time outside the home, but I could pretend). My issue was that embarrassed as I was to admit it, I was ambivalent about cooking. Sometimes I got really excited, and I would start cutting out recipes furiously and inviting loads of people over for the weekend and dishing out five or six course meals. At other times, I just wanted to pop a chicken in the oven over a bed of orzo/couscous or the like, spice it up, and be done with it, or better yet, pick up a pound of turkey breast and a loaf of rye from the deli and call that dinner. True entertaining with all the trimmings was a whole lot of work and just tired me out sometimes. It seemed like living in suburbia you were expected to invite your neighbors and friends over all the time and produce big, lavish meals. It seemed to be the price you paid here to maintain your social life. I wondered if many of us secretly wished we could just buy a couple of barbeque chickens, roasted potatoes and coleslaw, with an apple pie from the local bakery, serve it up on some nice china, and be done with it. Until then, we suburbanites will just roll up our sleeves, snip those recipes, and attack those deckels until we get them right.

11

Dreaming of Hawaii

I felt like I was going to explode. How did people survive here in the winter? I was staring outside the window at the blustery snow that had blanketed the streets for what seemed like the hundredth time that winter. I wondered when winter would end. The snow and the cold made me feel so trapped. What did people do in suburbia when it snowed like this for weeks on end? There was no one outside. Everyone seemed to be hiding in their homes. They could have all moved to Arizona for all I knew—all their houses had snow-covered exteriors and their shades were drawn. People told me I should live in Alaska or Canada for a few years and northern New Jersey winters would seem like nothing compared to that, but as far as I was concerned, when you get to eighteen degrees (the current temperature on my thermometer), ten degrees is not much different. To me, it was freezing; my bones felt cold, and I just felt cold.

Swimming, jogging, walking, hiking, boating, biking, fishing… all the wonders of warm weather were but a dream, and we were stuck in one of the worst winters in decades where all you could see was a white blanket of snow everywhere you looked. I didn't know how we would survive this, year in, year out, and stay sane. The power of forgetfulness must be so great that come March when spring is upon us and the air warms up just the slightest bit and you can go outside your home, which has been your hiding place for the last six months, suddenly everything seems right again, and life takes on a "worth living" feel, and you forget the difficult winter you just endured. You go outside and cherish the fresh air and the fresh grass breaking through, and you put the past behind you. It's like a yearly trauma that we up north endure each winter with no end in sight until retirement, when we've paid our dues and we can legitimately move to Florida and finally thaw.

Sometimes I think our ancestors made a terrible mistake when they landed on the northeast shores of New York, New Jersey, and the like. Why couldn't their boats veer slightly more south as they made their way across the sea and land us in Georgia or Florida instead? Then we'd all be basking in the sun year round and turning into raisins instead of torturing ourselves each year in the blustery, bone-chilling cold, trying our hardest to keep warm but always feeling the chill cut through our bones.

In an attempt to face the wretched Northeast winters, I have developed a coat fetish. My husband is not too happy about this because I take up most of the coat closet with my broad array of outerwear and leave little room for his two coats, which are pushed into the corner. I have a different coat or jacket for every five degree difference in temperature, with the warmest coats being my down coat and a shearling for when it gets below thirty. But sometimes even that's not enough.

I get through most winters by going to Florida for a week or two sometime in January. I absolutely adore Florida. I go there when it's frigid and icy in New Jersey and come back feeling renewed and recharged, like I was given a new lease on life. It helps me face the rest of winter and somehow get through. I always laugh when I'm in Florida because wherever you go, people are having the identical conversations. It's either "When did you arrive?" and

"When are you leaving?" ("Leave me alone," I feel like saying. "I just got here"). Or they'll be discussing how they just spoke to some brother, sister, or uncle in New York and it's snowy and icy and twenty two degrees outside and here they're walking outside on the boardwalk with a t-shirt and sandals in seventy-nine degree weather and the water is turquoise and magnificent. It just makes you feel a little bit better.

I often do wish my ancestors had landed there instead of the Lower East Side, because now my family is all up north and that keeps me here. I would just miss them too much if I picked up and moved away. I keep a glass jar of sand from Florida on my desk at work filled with sea shells that I picked while walking on the shore, and I'll stare at it for a few minutes each day. Knowing that there's a place like Florida that I can run off to for a few weeks and experience a different reality for a little while helps make the winter just a little more tolerable.

12

Furniture Junkie

It's springtime once again and you know what that means—out with the old and in with the new. Everywhere you look people are throwing out what appears to be perfectly good furniture and assorted household items to make way for the new stuff. If you happen to have a minivan or truck, you can pick up some really great finds right on your neighborhood sidewalks. I get excited as I drive to work every day and see perfectly respectable piles of bikes that, with a little love (i.e. replacing wheels, spokes, screws, and handlebars), can be made new again. I picked up a Little Tikes Cozy Coupe car for my son this way, and after they sent me a whole box of replacement parts, it was perfectly suitable. I didn't realize initially how much the lack of a steering wheel would bother a two-year-old, but he kept on pointing to it and looking very befuddled. I ended up replacing the steering wheel as well as the gas cap and stickers so it should look somewhat respectable (and shelling out thirty dollars), and my son was happy as ever with his new ("ish") set of wheels.

My two-year-old would get into his car and drive around, all the while schlepping my ten-month-old behind him, who was holding on for dear life to the back of the car, and the two would have a jolly old time. This worked until my two-year-old would forget that he had a passenger hanging off his back bumper and start zooming around my basement as if he was a NASCAR driver, leaving my ten-month-old in the dust kicking and screaming and flailing his arms at the unfairness of it all. I kept on thinking, *Just you wait, big guy. A few years from now, when your little brother catches up to you in size, he will pick you up with one hand and race off in the car by himself.*

Needless to say, I love garage sales, moving sales, and flea markets. Unfortunately, my husband and I do not see eye-to-eye on this. He felt the stuff on the street had no potential at all and that's why it's called "trash." I, on the other hand, could find potential in almost anything. I kept thinking to myself, *If he thinks I'm bad, he should have met my roommate from back in the day, who decorated our apartment with stuff she found on the street.* An interior decorator would have been impressed. I must admit that the end result was quite beautiful.

The truth is, I wasn't always a furniture junkie. Before college, I too embraced the new and shunned anything junky—especially other people's junk —but thanks to my roommate Rachel, I learned to see the potential in other people's throwaways. I admit that the fact that we were all living on a shoestring budget helped draw me in to the whole shabby chic endeavor.

Flashback: its twelve thirty at night, and I'm sitting on the couch cutting out a flower-shaped stencil from the top of a shoebox. Mind you, it's my vacation, the last few days before my courses begin again, and I had dreams of being in bed by eleven thirty at the latest every night. What I'm sitting on isn't actually a couch, but rather an old futon covered with a beautiful piece of light purple fabric with colored fringes coming off the sides (it looked like the kind of thing you would see in the flea market and say, "Hmm … I wonder who buys these things. It's nice, but don't people have enough stuff to clutter their houses with?). The fabric actually made a really beautiful couch covering. My roommate had placed two navy pillows, one on each side of the futon, and a dark purple, navy, and yellow printed fabric draped across the middle (it actually looked like my grandmother's—could it be—shawl?). She then added two bumper pillows, each in a darker shade of purple, to each side, and it all came together in this incredible ensemble, all from things she'd collected from the street. She used this old, rickety futon, which had come with the apartment, and in my opinion was ready for the county dump, and turned it into a beautiful, eye-catching living room highlight.

I thoroughly enjoyed the transformation that my living room had undergone, since the previous year the apartment had been basically bare except for the hideous futon. So that's why I was sitting up at twelve thirty in the morning cutting out stencils. My roommate would use the stencils to paint another found-in-the-Dumpster cupboard that would eventually be transformed into an absolutely amazing piece. This had all started the previous week. I had walked into our apartment after a long day at school to discover this wreck sitting in the middle of the living room. It was up there on the Most Atrocious Furniture list, and it was sitting upside down in the middle of our floor. One of its legs was so rotten that the wood looked like it would blow away if you blew on it. My immediate thought was, *What is this hideous monstrosity doing in the middle of my living room? What did she bring me home this time, and how fast can I get rid of it?* I could think of no possible future for it, except back in the garbage where it had come from and where it rightfully belonged. My roommate had informed me that since it was the beginning of a new year, everyone was throwing out their old furniture to make way for the new. (*Who actually does this?* I wondered. *Do people actually say, 'It's a new year, time for a new dress, new shoes, and new breakfront?' I know I don't*). I personally get very attached to my belongings and have great difficulty parting with them. In addition, I have quite a difficult time making drastic changes to my living quarters by adding new things. If I'm happy with how things are, I pretty much want them to stay the way they are, which is why I was having minor conniptions as I entered the apartment and was greeted by this huge throwaway in my living room—with rotten legs, no less.

Anyway, she informed me that because people were throwing out their less-than-perfect furniture during their New Year's clean-up, you could pick up beautiful stuff on the street (otherwise known as "junk") for nothing. I was a little less than enthusiastic. My idea of decorating at that point in my life was big open spaces, beautiful shiny floors, fresh clean walls, and a small couch, armchair, and coffee table pushed as far to the wall as possible. I preferred the open, uncluttered look and the idea of bringing home lots of furniture to invade my open space scared me. My roommate, in direct opposition to me, was absolutely thrilled with the idea of transforming other people's throwaways into our treasures, and since she was new to the apartment and I wanted to get the relationship off to a good start, I listened and played along as much as I could bear. One day she went so far as to draw me an in-detail diagram of our neighborhood (including pizza stores, corner groceries, etc.), leading me with a gigantic X-marks-the-spot to a piece of furniture she wanted me to check out that she thought would be perfect in the apartment. She explained to me that it would probably reach to the ceiling (my ceilings were about ten feet high) and would jut out about three feet from the wall. But, she informed me, if it was placed in the corner right in front of the computer table, it would make an adorable computer nook and wouldn't take up that much space in the actual room. Here I put my foot down. "No," I said. What I actually meant was "*No!* We are not bringing a ten-foot-by-three-foot cabinet into this living room, which is beginning to feel so cluttered I think I'll have to cordon myself off in a little area with rope so that I can have somewhere to sit. She finally got the message and let it go.

As for this new addition, the broken-leg monstrosity that she had managed to drag into our apartment, which I stared at with my mouth agape, my roommate quickly assured me it would look perfect in the room as she rushed out of her room with two big buckets of purple paint. She pointed to exactly where she thought it should go. I said, "What about the legs?" She turned the thing over so it was right side up, gave it two big kicks, and seeing that it didn't collapse to the ground in a big heap said, "They'll be fine." I finally agreed to let her keep this new treasure, but since I was much more conservative, I said, "I want it white." She said, "Purple." I said, "White." We went back and forth, and finally she said, "Fine, white, but with yellow flowers stenciled across the top." So that's how I ended up cutting out flowered stencils past midnight on my vacation. I finally went to bed after handing her my shoebox stencils, and the last thing I thought about before dozing off was why I hadn't just agreed to purple. I had dreams of waking up to this chest in the middle of my living room with psychedelic yellow daisies painted across the top and would need eye-shields every time I walked by. I didn't sleep very well that night.

I awoke the next morning at seven and gingerly walked to the living room, holding my breath and hoping I could stand the thing. Actually, I loved it. I really did. The first thing I could shriek was "Rachel, you're a genius. I absolutely love it." But she was sound asleep, as she had stayed up until two in the morning painting the poor thing. So I kept quiet, not wanting to wake her. The chest stood proudly at the side of our living room shiny white and upright with fine, pale-yellow flowers printed in a neat line across the top with one on each side, and it was absolutely beautiful.

So today, many years later, I thank Rachel for converting me into a furniture junkie and helping me to never look at other people's trash quite the same way again. Now I just have to get my husband to come around.

13

Birthdays and More

We just got through my son's birthday party, and my son, who is all of one year old, got a portable mp3 player. "Ages and stages: Birth +" is what it read on the box. The box also advertises in big bright letters, "Download and create your own mp3 playlists." I don't even know how to download playlists, but my son is going to be downloading like a pro. The party guests just left, and I have that after-the-party-let-down-feeling where you're looking at all the presents and wondering how you made out. The truth is, my son made out like a little bandit, but I'm sitting here wondering what it would do for his personal sense of happiness and fulfillment in life to have received an mp3 player at one year of age. Where do you go from there—a Ferrari or a Lamborghini for your bar mitzvah, a beach house for your sweet sixteen?

In addition to the mp3 player, my son got two Elmo dolls with big pop-out eyes on top of their heads, and the first thing he did was try and eat up the eyes—yum, yum. He put the first Elmo doll's eyes in his mouth one at a time and they fit perfectly. He seemed to find them very tasty, and he looked rather pleased with himself.

The second Elmo doll had smaller eyes, and he didn't seem quite as interested in them. After putting them in his mouth, he discarded the doll and went searching for bigger and better things to suck on, like his pacifier, which he tried to dig out from under the couch.

The kid looked positively overwhelmed. He was sitting in the middle of dozens of gifts (he's the firstborn) and when we gave him a pretty wrapped package to open, he would shake it and then run for cover, as if to say, "*Help* … get me out of here … give me some Cheerios."

Sometimes I fear that, if this is how we start them off, where do they go from here? Will they eventually come to expect this? And how can we ever realistically meet their needs if it takes more and more to satisfy them? Will that elusive joy we all search for in life just

keep moving farther and farther away, so that it becomes increasingly difficult for them to attain any real measure of happiness? I wonder if our happiness has kept pace with all our possessions, and if our children will be any happier because of all the things they've been able to acquire at such a young age. I wonder when the consumeristic culture that affects all of us through the media will come to a head. How do you keep your kids mentally healthy in this affluent society when five-year-olds are asking for iPods for Hanukkah? One friend of mine calls it "affluenza," for despite transient economic downturns and recessions, we, as a nation, are still the wealthiest and most possession-rich nation in the world.

I wonder how to set boundaries for my own kids, so they will learn how to have a healthy amount of desire and yearning for things, but not too much. With all the possessions, they might forget what it means to truly want something and work to get it. I thought of limiting the gifts that they get for their birthdays to only practical things that will actually get used and won't just clutter up the house. For example, one year tell everyone to bring clothes as birthday gifts, the next year books, the next year maybe a small donation toward something they're saving up for that they really want. I know personally how hard it is to shop for birthday gifts in a have-have society and don't want to put undue pressure on my friends and family to come up with exciting gifts year after year. Mostly, I don't want my kids to come to expect it and then be disappointed if the gifts don't meet their expectations, which they often won't. I don't want them to grow up spoiled, where they have so much that nothing pleases them. I want them to appreciate the little things in life, and the value of putting money aside, and the feeling of empowerment that comes with working toward something step by step.

And then there is the birthday party itself. Everyone is trying to outdo each other and come up with an even greater idea or theme for their child's party. The whole thing becomes one enormous, pressure-filled competition with people getting all stressed about their children's birthday parties months before the actual date, trying to come up with the greatest idea that will have everyone oohing and aahing. They'll rent out martial arts studios and dance studios. They'll higher bird trainers and lion tamers. I saw a group of girls in the mall. They looked no older than five years old, participating in a ballet-themed party at a store that sold ballet clothing and paraphernalia. The store had been rented out for the afternoon, and the girls were all dressed in these adorable pink and black tutus, and a ballet instructor was teaching them some dance steps, all for the little girl's birthday. The birthday girl looked like she'd rather be almost anywhere else. Someone I know whose son was obsessed with Diego hired a six-and-a-half foot Diego "character" to come to her son's third birthday party. The child looked absolutely terrified as this monstrous cartoon character approached him and tried to dance with him. The birthday boy started yelling, "I don't like Diego in my house. I only like Diego on TV." Yeah, when Diego is three inches tall on the screen he's pretty cute, but when he walks through your door and towers over everyone else, he looks rather menacing. The parents had to shell out a small fortune for Diego's grand entrance and then quickly usher him out the door.

It's a hard balance that we as parents strive for. We all want what is best for our kids. We don't want them to feel deprived, like their friends have all the cool stuff and they have little more than a toy chest full of last year's rejects; on the other hand, neither do we want to give in to their every whim so they end up spoiled and unhappy. We need to work on developing our children's self-esteem and self-satisfaction so they don't feel they need everything they see. Rather, they can see something at a friend's house or on TV that they might want but feel it's okay not to have it. They have other things that they like, and they can appreciate and derive pleasure from those things.

14

It's All about Human Nature

I finally got a second car. No! Not for me; this car is for my one-and-a-half-year-old. After six months of watching my two-and-a-half and one-and-a-half-year-old slug it out over our one Little Tykes Cozy Coupe car, one pulling the other out of the car so they could get a turn at the wheel, I decided I had had enough and went out and bought a second set of wheels for them. The way I figured it, the younger one would inherit the older car, and I would give the new car I purchased to my older son. They could sit side by side in the backyard in their spiffy red and yellow vehicles, honking the horn, filling up for gas, and would be as happy as kids can be. I debated a long time before I decided to get the second set of wheels. "After all," my mother said when I discussed the issue with her, "if you buy them two cars, you'll have to buy them two of everything." Kids quarrel over everything was her thinking, and whatever the other is playing with suddenly looks a thousand times better than what they had been playing with two seconds before, and they'll immediately forget about what's in their hands and run over to check out the other one's toys. So I may as well go out and buy two bikes, two computers, two shopping carts, doll carriages, televisions—because one wants to watch Barney and the other Dora the Explorer. While I'm at it, I may as well buy two tubs because no matter how big your bathtub is, kids will inevitably start splashing each other and stretching themselves out to the full length of the tub so the other kid, usually the smaller one, is smashed in the corner.

My mother felt that sharing is an essential thing that kids need to learn, and having one of each toy would promote that. So keep to only one car, and they'll learn lots of developmentally important skills like sharing, taking turns, and patience. The more they share, the more they would develop a sense of caring and concern for each other, as they would be forced to take into consideration someone else's needs, not just their own. I believed all of this was very important and true, but sometimes, as a mother, your sanity takes precedence. Having two toddlers hollering at each other as each tries to regain control of the one set of wheels can really throw you over the edge, so please forgive me, parenting experts; I caved in and bought a second car.

I brought it home and spent hours furiously assembling it, as these seemingly innocuous cars come with about forty steps of instructions. At one point I was required to take out my electric drill to get a screw through three pieces of plastic while I contorted myself at some very strange angle and practically had to wave the drill above my head. (This was nothing compared to their toy kitchen, which took me and my husband a week to assemble, and came with about one hundred steps of instructions. I read online that people had actually given up midway and just packed the whole thing back in the box and taken it back to the store because the emotional stress of following these tedious instructions was enough to send one to a psychiatric facility.) Eventually, I got the job done, and the car was completed. I presented the brand-new car to my older son the next day when he woke up and what I expected to happen was I would finally have the peace and quiet I had been dreaming about. I would sit on my lounge chair in the backyard and watch my two sons in their vehicles roaming around with all sorts of important missions they needed to accomplish. When they grew bored, I'd make up all sorts of pretend "errands" for them to do, such as getting me bread from the supermarket, picking up a pizza, or getting me a book from the library. They'd be happy with their new vehicles, and I'd be thrilled with the noise level, which was sure to come down a few hundred decibels.

Now for what really happened. I brought out the new car and presented it to my older son. I then gave my younger son the old car, which he had been absolutely thrilled with the day before. Guess what happened? My younger son took one look at my older son's updated model, replete with big plastic eyes, a smile across the front, and newer, spiffier lines, and suddenly he was no longer excited with his car. He ran to my older son's car and wanted that one. There you go—human nature! What you've got is perfectly adequate until someone comes along with something newer and better, and suddenly what you have doesn't seem so wonderful anymore. You'll buy the house of your dreams and love it until your neighbor comes along and builds a huge monstrosity twice the size, and suddenly you feel like you're living in the guest house. The house you once loved starts to feel cramped and outdated, and you secretly start planning for the addition. You buy a new watch for your birthday and love it until someone comes along with the higher end model with diamonds around the face, and suddenly your watch looks kind of shabby. Human nature—what can you do about it? The Sages teach that "Rich is he who is happy with what he has." Just don't look at your neighbors' cars, houses, or jewels. Concentrate instead on the riches and blessings you have right in your own backyard, because we all have plenty. Life is so fleeting it doesn't pay to waste your energy being unhappy. Rather, savor and embrace your gifts and blessings and be grateful for them. We have to train ourselves to look inward at our own fortunes, remember how happy they used to make us feel, and try to recapture that feeling once again. With a little effort we can bring back that initial excitement and learn to relish the things we have, without having them be diminished because someone we know has something bigger, shinier, or newer. How much happier we'd all be if we could just take that little lesson to heart. But now I have to get back to my sons, who have tackled each other to the ground over their toy cars, and try to work on instilling in them this all-important lesson.

15

Traveling with Tots

Whoever invented the term "family vacation" must have been on hallucinogens, either LSD, PCP, or mushrooms, because those two words simply do not go together in the same sentence. I can't believe I'm actually saying this, but after a few days of our "family vacation" in Miami, Florida, I actually began dreaming of my bed in New Jersey. Maybe that's why I had to go: to begin to relish what I have back home. I dreamt of living out of drawers and closets and not carry-ons and suitcases. I dreamt of walking down the street with my two arms swinging freely and carelessly by my side and not holding a hollering two-year-old who was refusing to sit under one arm while pushing his oversized carriage with the other. (Don't get me wrong—I love my kids dearly, but they're hard work!) I dreamt of what it would be like to not eat muffins for two meals a day and a turkey roll sandwich for the third, but rather some good, old-fashioned, healthy, homemade food. Mostly, I fantasized about what it would be like to have one decent night of uninterrupted sleep, seven to eight hours of delicious, undisturbed rest, without being woken up at five in the morning by a toddler who doesn't care for his surroundings or who decided it is already morning and he wants his cereal. Or having to get up at four to catch a 7:00 am flight, which we didn't make (I learned from that experience never to schedule 7:00 am flights with babies—it just doesn't happen). I am not sure what I was thinking when I scheduled my flights. I was probably trying to save a few dollars and maximize my vacation time by arriving at my destination early, but getting yourself, your spouse, and two kids dressed and out of the house by 4:00 am is stretching the realm of human possibility. Your kids will be disoriented and not know if it's day or night, and you will be walking around bleary-eyed for the next two days trying to catch up on the sleep you missed. It's hard enough taking care of yourself when you are exhausted; try watching two overtired hyenas who don't know if they're coming or going at the same time.

I knew I was in trouble when my mother-in-law banged on my door at five thirty on the morning we were supposed to leave (she was staying over that night), and we were still sleeping soundly. We had set the alarm clock for 4:00 AM, and we had slept right through it. Unless we violated every traffic rule ever recorded, we would not make it in time to the airport to catch our 7:00 AM flight. Needless to say, even with the taxi driver driving like a NASCAR driver, we didn't make our flight, which left us entertaining our kids in the airport for four hours before they could get us on another one.

Once on the plane, we split up; I took the one-year-old, who shared a seat with me, and my husband took our two-year-old. My son spent the duration of the flight yanking out the hair of the passenger in front of me, which left the poor man with a painful bald spot and a not-too-happy disposition. When he wasn't doing that, he'd kick the seat in front of me using my stomach as a springboard. I tried putting my son on the floor, and he proceeded to crawl under the seat in front of me and pull at everyone's legs. My son ripped up all the magazines and safety pamphlets, and when he was done with that, he played cymbals with the seatbelts, giving me and everyone around me a booming headache. I got some dirty looks from the people sitting in the next row, who probably have never taken kids on a plane. The looks said something like, "Why don't you put your kid in a straightjacket, or put him in a cage or something." I got some sympathetic looks too, from those who had probably been in the same predicament once upon a time.

The woman who had the unfortunate luck of sitting in the aisle seat right next to me was the kindest and most understanding of all. She said she had four kids and was sympathetic to my son emptying out the contents of her pocketbook. She was enormously helpful to me and actually placed her feet like two pillars on the floor blocking the exit, so that my son could only crawl up, down, in front and in-between our seats but not up and down the aisles. I was deeply grateful for the flight attendant who understood as well, stating that she had two sons who were a year apart. When they were babies, her husband did service in Iraq and she'd fly alone with them. I asked her how she managed, and she said, "Don't think about it—just do it. Just hang in there until they're old enough to be company for each other (hers were now twelve and thirteen), and it gets easier."

Eventually I tried to feed him yogurt, thinking it would keep him calm and help pass the time, but most of the yogurt ended up flying across the floor while he used the rest to paint his shirt. When it was time to exit the plane, someone walked by and, thinking he was doing me a service, kindly pointed out that I should be careful exiting as yogurt had spilled out around my seat. I played dumb: "Oh really! Thanks for letting me know," and proceeded to gather my stuff.

We rented an apartment for the week while down in Florida, and my two-year-old left a trail of mass destruction. He smashed everything that wasn't nailed to the ground. He took closets off their tracks. He took Formica off the table. He got hold of a pen and started decorating the walls, and when I turned around to grab the Fantastic to clean up the mess, he got hold of a red crayon and colored over it. I bought a Magic Eraser, which is supposed to clean pen, paint, and the like off walls, but what they don't tell you is that sometimes, if the walls are old, it takes the walls off with it. We left the walls with some pretty sad-looking streak marks across them—modern art courtesy of my two-year-old. I think we were black-listed on the vacation rental Web sites. If you see us coming, close the shades and darken the lights; don't let that family within two hundred yards of your apartment if you want your apartment to survive. I spent the duration of my vacation at the local Walgreens, purchasing all sorts of household items so I could repair the things my children had broken. I had recurring panic attacks the entire trip, thinking about returning the apartment (which looked like it had been struck by a monsoon) to its rightful owner. I sat up most of the night before we were supposed to leave with a bottle of Fantastic in one hand and a rag in the other, cleaning every inch of space in the apartment so it would look as clean as possible. I was so anxious the whole week thinking about how I had to return the apartment to its rightful owner in perfect condition that I barely enjoyed myself. Who was I kidding? I was traveling with two babies. I would have to settle on leaving the apartment with a "Beirut-in-combat" type of effect and give up on any notion of perfection. It's no wonder that my friend refers to family vacations as family "relocations," because thus far I wasn't having much of a vacation at all. As a matter of fact, I kept thinking to myself, *When will the fun begin?*

We took the kids to a fancy restaurant (mistake #1) that charged fifty dollars for a buffet. My problem is that if I'm paying that much money, I feel I have to eat my money's worth of food, so I ended up filling up my plate three times and feeling sick afterward. The woman next to me looked like a toothpick on a diet, and she filled up her plate with carrot sticks. You don't come to a restaurant to eat carrot sticks! I just couldn't believe it. I personally finished a huge plate of salad, then went for double helpings of salmon, and then started on my plate of ribs. The woman next to me gingerly ate her carrot sticks and then debated whether or not to get a piece of salmon. She finally decided to go for it and brought over a desert plate with a piece of salmon that I needed a magnifying glass to see.

Halfway through the meal, my son started banging his chopsticks together. Mrs. "Carrot Stick," shall we call her, went livid and said, "It's time to stop that." I felt like answering, "Stop what?" but the truth was I felt bad for her. She probably thought she'd have a nice, relaxing lunch with her family, and instead she got to spend lunch with us (on top of the fact that she gave up an absolutely incredible plate of ribs).

16

Changing Up the Monotony

One of the major problems I have with suburbia (though my husband, knowing me very well, said I would start to feel this anywhere I lived) is that I get bored here. There are only so many times I can go to ShopRite, Target, Gymboree, or the local parks with my kids. Eventually, I feel the need to break free and do something different. Not drastically different, like parasailing or bungee jumping, but different than the routine existence my life seems to have taken on living here. I've never been one for routines, always liking to travel to new countries, see new movies, and take in the latest plays, anything to change up the routine a bit. People used to tell me before I had kids, "Once you have kids, you won't go anywhere." When I had one kid and I still traveled, they would say, "Just wait until you have two kids; then you definitely won't go anywhere." I traveled when I had one kid, carting that poor kid on and off planes, into and out of Pack 'n Plays all over the country, and now I travel when I have two kids as well. I admit, it takes more out of you, and you can't expect them to tag along behind you like two obedient puppies and keep up with your pace. They need to be diapered, fed, and clothed multiple times a day, and they usually have a way of deciding that two o'clock in the morning is a good time to wake you up and request a cup of apple juice. If you can overlook these minor nuisances, then you're ready to travel with kids.

This summer, we decided to visit the Hamptons. Having never been there before, and hearing how amazing it was from everyone who has spent a weekend there, I felt it was something I wanted to do. Yes, I had two kids in tow, but that didn't have to stop me, or so I thought.

My husband and I booked a large one bedroom in a bed and breakfast, which was our first mistake. You don't want to be sleeping with two kids under the age of three in the same bedroom as you—especially when you are trying to have some semblance of a vacation. They'll decide to wake you up every two hours with all sorts of interesting comments and requests, i.e. I'm thirsty, I'm hungry, I'm hot, I'm cold, I want my "baby" or pacifier, whereas at home, they'd been sleeping through the night for months. Then at five thirty in the morning, just when you are starting to fall into a deep sleep, they'll wake up and decide they are ready to start their day. The only problem is, it's the Hamptons, and everyone on your floor is in their twenties and has been out partying until 3:00 am the previous night and plans to sleep until noon. So your two kids being up and making a mini-ruckus at such an early hour doesn't go over very well. Your neighbors in the rooms around you start banging on the walls hoping you'll get the message, which adds to the preexisting babbling and cacophony already going on inside your room. Needless to say, your kids don't get the hint. Kids have needs and can be slightly self-absorbed when it comes to those needs, and no amount of adult pleading can sway them from their single-minded goals. They were hungry and ready for breakfast, but breakfast wasn't being served until 8:00 am, more than two hours from now. *What in tarnation will I do with these kids for over two hours?* you think to yourself. You decide to stuff them with crackers that you brought along for the trip (being a seasoned traveler with kids, you know to pack a storehouse of food when going anywhere with them, and enough toys, cars, and crayons to fill a small warehouse.). Once they're properly fed with crackers and apple juice, you quickly get them dressed and take them out for a walk. You go outside and suddenly realize the Hamptons must be built on a swamp because there are two gazillion mosquitoes out and ready to have their breakfast —you and your kids. I must've gotten fifty mosquito bites in a span of ten minutes. I was so itchy I wanted to pull my skin off—poison ivy couldn't have felt worse. I was slapping them left, right, and center, and they wouldn't go away. My poor kids were getting eaten up as well. My older son kept saying, "Me getting ouchy," which was terribly cute, but he was almost in tears when he said it. The synagogue we went to over the weekend even had containers of OFF! available in the courtyard to spray at your leisure; that's how bad the mosquito situation was. Our walk lasted ten minutes before I took them back inside our room and tried to quiet them down. There, I had one hour and fifty minutes left before breakfast. Traveling with tots was turning out to be a lot less glamorous than I had anticipated. Yes, I was looking for things to spice up my life in suburbia, and the Hamptons seemed to offer the perfect weekend getaway, but maybe this was a little too adventurous, even for me.

The Hamptons is a really fun place, but if you've got young children, you might want to try a more kid-friendly spot. While I was there, I went out one evening with a single friend to a local cafe, but kept looking at my watch and eventually excused myself and said I had to get home. After all, with a five thirty wake up call from the kiddies, there was nothing fun about staying out late and feeling like I was walking through a heavy fog all the next day. After a while you come to the realization that staying up late just isn't worth it. Either that or I'm just getting old. You start to realize that going out with your buddies and having fun 'till the wee hours of the morning means the next day you will be a walking zombie. If your kids, like mine, are early risers, you will end up feeling tired and irritable the whole day, and you'll soon come to the conclusion that you're better off just staying home. So there go your nights out. Instead, you're in bed by nine until the kids are off to college. You'll just have to find ways to "change it up" closer to home.

The fact of the matter is, even though I resist it, having kids requires a lifestyle adjustment. You just can't party hardy until 3:00 am like you did back in your single days, unless you don't mind walking into walls the next day. Kids just do that to you. They are needy and somehow can't be ignored and even for the free-spirited among us, some adjustments have to be made. Life may not be as spicy or exciting as it used to be (painting picture frames at the fourth children's birthday party you've attended in a month doesn't compare to a night rocking in the Hamptons), but those cute little faces jumping into your bed in the morning make it all worth it. And I guess we can always go back to the Hamptons when the kids are all grown up and out of the house. But by then we may be old enough to be the town chaperones.

17

The First Day of School

I didn't think it would happen to me. I just wasn't one of those mothers who got choked up on the first day of school. I'm not the super-emotional type. I don't cry at movies. I don't get all misty at first birthdays or first haircuts. I'm more cerebral, or practical—or so I'd like to think. Frankly, I don't know what came over me when I drove my son to his first day of school. My little toddler, now two-and-a-half years old, got out of the car sporting his new backpack (he had been wearing it for two weeks straight; he watched television with it, ate dinner with it, and would sleep with it if I let him), and I started tearing up. There's something so heartwarming and almost painfully sweet about seeing your child go off to school for the first time. You think the little guy, still in diapers, and still using a pacifier at night (he calls it his "baby" because we keep on insisting that only babies use pacifiers) will be your little baby forever. You think he will still be speaking gobbledy gook, most of which you can decipher, but some of it which still makes no sense at all to you, playing with his trucks, and needing you for most everything for some time still. Of course, you want him to grow up, and you don't want him to be stuck as your little toddler, but somehow it all happened too fast. You were so busy protecting him, shielding him from the world, from twelve hour workdays and homework and teachers. But there he is, climbing the steps of the preschool where he will be spending the next ten months, eager as can be, with a look of excitement and not a trace of worry as he embarks on the next stage of his life.

You follow him inside the school, and the teacher is warm and wonderful, and you feel a little more at ease since you are leaving him in good hands. You see him looking happy as he peruses the new toys and freshly painted play area and eyes the other kids as they start filtering in. You wonder what's going through his mind. You know what's going through your mind—about half the kids were being dropped off by nannies. This was twenty-first century parenting at its finest. Every kid comes equipped with a sippy cup, a shiny new pair

of shoes, and a nanny. I had specifically rearranged my work schedule that day and made sure to be there for my kid's first day of school. It was one of his biggest milestones, as well as mine as a mother. Secretly I was really hoping to meet other moms and try to develop some social connections in the class, but with all the other mothers missing in action, a newfound friendship did not seem possible.

Throughout my last two years living in suburbia, I have been told frequently by many more established women in the community when I confided in them that sometimes I found it difficult to find "my group," that once my kids started school I would begin socializing with the other mothers, and that all would change. I would finally find a social niche and would have an easier time adjusting to life here. We would have our kids' teachers, schools, and class schedules in common and that would lead more naturally to establishing friendships with these women than simply sitting next to them in the park, introducing myself, and seeing them again in a week. So I must admit, it was a little disappointing when I arrived that first day and a lot of the mothers were noticeably absent. I'm all for nannies and babysitters. I have one myself. A working woman whose parents and in-laws don't live nearby can hardly function without one, but I just felt it was a little sad that on the first day of school so many of the mothers were not around. I think work is a great thing and many women need it for their mental health or for more basic reasons, like financial ones, but certain things, I believe, take precedence. If at all possible, a mom should try to do some shifting in her work schedule to be there for important milestones in her kids' lives. (Yes, as a working mother, I am sympathetic to the fact that "being there" is not always possible, but I think we still all need to try. I will add that in cases where a father's work schedule is more flexible, then he can be the one to share these important milestones instead).

Well, there goes my little boy. He's happy as can be, playing with the other kids, and has already forgotten that I'm in the room.

I tell him good-bye and edge out the door, leaving him to grow and learn and play and enter the next phase of his life. It's hard for me as a mom to see it happen, but I know this is what I want for him, and I have to let go. I have to let go of the little baby who needed me for everything and let him become the boy and one day the man he needs to be.

18

Carpooooooling

It was pouring rain outside, the kind of gushing rain where you have to lick your hair off your nose and you dream of crawling back into bed. It was the kind of torrential downpour where everything was just one bleak, gray existence, and you felt like a cold, soggy mess. It was the kind of day where you look out of your bedroom window and you can barely see two feet out, and you remind yourself, *Ouch, it's my turn to do carpool.* Then you fall into a state of utter despair at having ever agreed to move out to the boondocks where the authorities take half your income for taxes but are too cheap to send a school bus down your street. Instead, mothers had to be reinvented as car service drivers, spending hundreds of valuable hours each year shuttling thousands of noisy, messy, greasy and heavy kids—yes, back-breaking and herniated disc-exacerbating heavy—to and from school. You'll see otherwise impeccably dressed, civil, and well-mannered women looking like bedraggled, bespectacled, and half-dressed hooligans hoisting thirty- to forty-pound kids plus at least ten pounds of boots, coats, hats, knapsacks, and other paraphernalia into and out of these massive minivans. Each minivan can be lined with as many as five gigantic car seats with incredibly difficult to maneuver five-point harnesses that every kid must be buckled into but barely fits into when wearing much more than a t-shirt. This happens for ten, sometimes twelve months a year, if you add day camp, without a break. I have to ask: Where are our taxes going? And why do smart and savvy women agree to turn over their freedom and sanity to the shackles of carpool?

Carpooling was unheard of where I grew up in Brooklyn. We had the Loneiro bus system, which I snuck onto for as long as I absolutely could, and then there was the beautiful New York City Transit system, consisting of busses and trains, whatever was closest to your house. The transit system was efficient, on time, and got you wherever you needed to go. You carried around this little bus pass in a plastic holder, flashed it at the bus driver, and voila, he or she let you on the bus, and you were off to school. Throughout most of elementary school, I'd walk to the corner every morning in rain, shine, sleet, or hail (or be walked by my mother when I was very young), and we'd wait for the big yellow Loneiro bus to come barreling down the street. If you were lucky, your parents paid a little extra money for the bus to come right up to your door. The bus driver would give one long beep, and no matter what stage of preparation you were in, you'd grab your backpack and head for that door. Usually you'd grab a granola bar or whatever you could find on the way out to fill you up. We always hoped our stop was close to the last one (or one of the earlier stops on the way home) so that we'd have a short bus ride to and from school, but generally speaking, big yellow bus rides were a pivotal part of my childhood. I learned how to sing all sorts of funny songs, establish my turf, trade stickers, and so on. After I passed a certain age, my parents knew very little about how I got to and from school. They had to go to work. I prepared myself, got my own breakfast, got my homework together, and got myself to school without asking them to haul me and four other people to and from school every day as if they were Olympian weight lifters. Nobody ever drove their own kids to school. What a ridiculous waste of womanpower (it's true—that's who it usually was).

I just never quite got this whole carpooling thing. Why is it mandatory that every woman (and sometimes man) in suburbia give up any hope of stable employment, or sleeping late, and stop whatever they happen to be doing at a certain time of day to become chauffeurs? Why is it that every woman must trade in her cute set of wheels once she has kids for a mammoth, lumbering minivan that makes her look like she's driving around a football team? I'm just not a fan of those things. There are not many ways to look cool and collected driving around in a eight-seater van, especially if there are five car seats stacked in there. Wouldn't it be more efficient all around if we could hire someone to bus our kids to and from school and we women, who are busy enough as it is, could get a few extra minutes to ourselves in the morning and not have to rush away from whatever we're doing in the morning and afternoon to shuttle half the neighborhood to and from school?

Then when you get to school, there's another whole saga to deal with. Drop-off isn't so bad. You unbuckle all your charges, and they pretty much go into the school building themselves. But pick-up can be a half-hour ordeal. Preschool lets out here at three thirty. Now you want to be either early (say three fifteen) or late (say three forty-five), because if you get there at three thirty, you wait in one of the two carpool lanes, which at that point probably has ten vans in line already, so you're going to have a pretty long wait to pick up your batch of kids. It will probably take you until about three forty-five anyway to get to the front of the line, so you might as well just show up then. Each van has a number, so you feel even more official and dorky driving around with a big number fourteen in your windshield. You get in the carpool line and a dispatcher reads the number off your van to another dispatcher inside the building where all the kids are being held. You edge your van up to the front of the line, and the dispatcher brings out the batch of kids that match your van number when you finally get to the front of the building. If you're early, you get to be one of the first vans on line and the process can go pretty quickly. If you're late, the process will also go pretty quickly, but your kids will come out with long, droopy, sad faces and guilt-trip you for the next week for letting them be the last kids left at school. You just can't win.

When your kids get older and their schedules get progressively more hectic (seriously, some of these kids' schedules would make the president's schedule look "light"), they'll need your "services" even more. They'll have soccer and hockey, gymnastics and football, baseball, tee-ball, horseback riding, wrestling, ballet, flower-making, pottery, and poetry, all of which they need rides to and from. All of this means—you guessed it—more carpooling. Yipppeee! Can't wait!

19

I'm a Shopaholic—There, I Said it!

I'm embarrassed to admit it, but it's true: I'm a shopaholic. One thing New Jersey can most definitely boast about is its vast array of malls. I have the Garden State Plaza, Paramus Park, and Bergen Town Center malls all within ten minutes of my house. If I want to venture another twenty or thirty minutes in my car, I have another ten malls to choose from. Then there's Paramus, which is like one gigantic mall. I would have been better off living somewhere where there was one bodega to buy all my groceries and the closest mall was a plane flight away. I guess I pretty much mean that I would have been better off being dropped on an island somewhere without any credit cards where there was nothing to buy from anybody, anywhere, except the barest essentials so I could feed my family and meet their basic needs. I mean it. I will buy anything from anybody, whether or not they're willing to sell it. I love gadgets, gizmos, and kitchen utensils. I have a French fry cutter, but I don't make French fries. I have two apple corers; one the core doesn't go through the middle and the other I can't take the core out of the middle. I have a mango cutter, too. When I go on vacation, I'm even worse. I bought two frogs made out of stones in St. Lucia off the side of a boat from a few vendors who came by traveling in little canoes trying to sell us their wares. I liked the hats they were wearing and was willing to buy them too, but they refused to part with them because they needed something to keep the sun out of their eyes.

I bought sunglasses in Toronto that broke on the trip home because they were so flimsy. I bought a metal turtle nightlight that's back was made out of colored glass and beamed a hundred colors

when you turned it on from a street vendor in New York City. I've bought clothes off mannequins and out of shop windows. I'll buy anything that's not nailed to the wall, and even then I'll ask the shopkeeper if I could pry it off the wall and purchase it if I like it enough.

If there's a sale, then I'm really in trouble. I'll go to a sale, come back with a whole bag full of goodies, and then try to convince my husband that I saved him money by buying all these things. I'll explain to him how spending money can actually save him money. He is still not convinced.

Shopping is just one big adrenaline rush, and if you're not doing heavy doses of cocaine or chugging down a six pack nightly, it is one of the few acceptable "impulses" out there that can still give you a high. Good shoppers go into a mall and suddenly they feel themselves switching gears to hyper-alert mode: their senses sharpen, their mind works quicker, their heart rates are up, their cheeks are flushed. I've never tried cocaine, but I imagine the rush is at least half as good. I went to the Garden State Plaza mall a few weeks ago. It happened to be three days before Passover and four days before Easter. The mall was brimming with people rushing to and fro, trying to find that perfect holiday outfit so they could look their best. I walked by one particular store, and my heart did a little dance as I spotted the perfect frilly, peach-colored blouse to go with my new white suit. The only problem was that it was on the mannequin. My husband pointed out that almost everything I own has ruffles or frills, and I think he's probably right. Despite that fact, I already knew that I needed this blouse. I envisioned how beautifully it would go with my new white suit, and I was already planning to match it with a pair of gold pumps and gold hoops to finish the look. I could feel the excited, nervous rush coming on. I had to make sure that absolutely no one else had spotted the mannequin wearing that blouse, because as I perused the shelves I realized she was wearing the last one remaining in my size. I made a quick scan of the store and saw I was safe; no one else was eyeing the blouse. Then I found a salesperson and explained how I'd like to have the mannequin's blouse. She thankfully agreed, having probably seen shoppers who can be as determined as me, and together we proceed to undress this six foot mannequin. I finally got my blouse and left the salesperson trying to pull some other shirt over the mannequin's head.

Now that I have kids, I love shopping for them, too. It's so much fun to peruse the racks and find the perfect matching outfits for the kids. So my younger son will be wearing the same outfit for five years; I hope he forgives me eventually. I love eyeing the fresh colors they come out with each season and the new ensembles with matching hats and all. Everything looks so inviting when it's on display, just begging to be had. Yeah, those white knickers with the pastel print tops will look great when I bring them home from the store, until my son takes his first plop into a dirt pile or my other son drips his cherry ice on it. At least it looked good in the bag.

The problem I find with shopping, which I imagine is why they've established Shoppers Anonymous groups for this particular "addiction," is that the high you get from finding that perfect blouse or that great pair of shoes at the perfect price doesn't last. You feel an incredible adrenaline rush when you make that purchase, which lasts until you hang it up in your closet. Then you go back to plain old you again, and all the fantasies you had attached to that particular article of clothing or other household item vanish like stardust, and you're left feeling pretty empty, so you have to go back to the store to do it all over again. My solution: write a book about it, or move away from New Jersey where there are way too many malls and way too many things to be had, and move to a kibbutz in Israel where everyone shares everything, including raising each other's kids. They even have to put their names on a list and choose wedding dates based on the one available wedding gown that gets passed around. It is really up to each one of us to eliminate that personal emptiness inside by making a determined effort to find meaningful and satisfying ways to fill it up, ways that don't include shopping. It will take some soul-searching and a huge helping of self-control, but I do believe that the shopaholics out there can find the strength to say no to the next purchase and find the self-discipline to create other more meaningful ways to attain that high.

Good luck finding it!

20

The Backyard

Soon after moving to suburbia, I realized that one of the great obsessions here is the backyard. You'll see men, after twelve-hour workdays, come home, gobble down supper, and go to the backyard to start their second job. There they plant, toil, sow the seed, and do all the things men used to do in 1200 BCE. My husband is constantly bringing home bags of soil and seed to patch up some small spot he perceives is not as lush as the rest of the lawn. I tell you, the saying, "The grass is always greener on the other side" was invented for the men of suburbia. My husband is constantly looking over at the guy's lawn next to us and wondering how he got his grass to be so green while ours looks like a bunch of yellow weeds. He's busy watering it, talking to our landscaper about adding more fertilizer, and cutting down trees so we can give the grass more sun and achieve that ultimate green patch of lawn that all men in suburbia hold up as a personal badge of manhood.

One day he came home with two trays of herbs, and pretty soon we had an herb garden growing back there. We even invested in bird feeders so that we could attract all the brightly-colored birds in town and have our very own estuary. I've seen men so busy with two feet of lawn; what they're doing I have no idea, but they do look busy.

I'm only interested in the fun aspect of the backyard. My first investment in our backyard was a hammock. When we purchased the house, I perused the backyard and quickly realized that we had two trees that were the perfect distance apart to hang a hammock between. This excited me to no end. I imagined sitting back on my hammock after a stressful day at work, staring up at the sky and watching the wind rustle through the leaves, and all would be well with the world. Then we got a barbeque for all those summer barbeques we planned to have. Then I put up a volley ball/badminton net and got assorted Frisbees in all sizes to play back there. We already had a swing set from the previous owners, so we were good with that. When I felt we had enough fun equipment, I felt the need to complete the look with lounge chairs. Over Father's Day, Target was running a sale on lounge chairs, but the only problem was everyone seemed to have gotten there before me. I finally had customer service locate two reclining lounge chairs in a store about thirty minutes away. I made a trip out there to pick up the last two reclining lounge chairs in what felt like all of New Jersey. They had a matching table to complete the look, so I picked one up as well. I set the chairs up in my backyard with the matching table in the middle. When my husband came home from running errands, I had him close his eyes, handed him a glass of ice tea, wished him happy Father's Day, and we both sat together on our matching Target recliners. For a few moments, we stared out at our suburban backyard, sipping glasses of iced tea, and all was well with the world.

21

Back to the Bungalows

Sitting out in my beautiful suburban backyard today, a wonderful August day, and relaxing on my lounge chair, I started thinking to myself, *The grass, the trees, the hammock, the swing set—this all reminds me of the bungalows I used to go to as a kid.* Despite the bugs, gnats, mosquitoes, wars over frogs, and the guys always stealing mine, I still have wonderful memories of those bungalows. Maybe that's why of all the seasons, I definitely enjoy my house best in the summertime.

For the first ten years of my life, my parents rented a bungalow up in the Catskill Mountains in upstate New York. This was the real deal. The places had one of a handful of catchy names that sounded so promising, such as Silver Lake or Spring Glen Estates or Luxury Gardens, but did not live up to expectations. I'm talking about hard-core bungalows that were packed so close together that if your neighbor's kid in the next bungalow passed gas, you knew about it. If the spouses were having a brawl, you knew about it. You knew what they were having for breakfast and what was in their pantry. They were not the gorgeous bungalows of today that are more appropriately called "summer homes," where people can go and truly feel like they are on a vacation. These places had linoleum floors circa 1920 in bright colors that matched the yellow flycatchers that hung all around you, which you tried not to get your hair caught up in. The floor was so tilted that you could drop a ball on one side of the bungalow and pick it up on the other side. The freezer had to be emptied and defrosted weekly. As soon as you completed this laborious task, the walls of the freezer would immediately accumulate ice again around the food, so you could barely stick in a pinky. The appliances were so old you prayed that they lasted until the end of the summer. Notwithstanding all of this, we kids still had tons of fun. I'm not sure about our poor mothers, who were stuck upstate in these cramped shacks all week without cars while our fathers worked in the city and came up for the weekends. They'd probably tell a different story. Our mothers' biggest excitement was seeing the station wagons pull up into the bungalow colony Thursday nights or Friday afternoons when they finally got to see their spouses, (and, I may add, grab the car so they can finally get off the grounds).

In these bungalows of old, the women sat around in circles where they shmoozed about pretty much everything in their lives. Eventually, they knew almost all there was to know about each other. They knew what the others made for dinners and what schedules everyone's kids were on. Half the time we ate our meals in each other's bungalows or did a shared meal on the picnic tables out front. They knew what the other's spouses liked and disliked. Let's just say they spent five or more hours a day talking and filling each other in on what they'd missed since the previous summer. By the end of the summer, there was little left to uncover.

When we first went to the bungalows, we didn't even have a phone in our bungalow, but rather a central phone that was housed in a little hut in the center of the colony. Whenever there was a call, there would be an announcement over the loudspeaker: "Mrs. So and

So, you have a phone call," which sent Mrs. So and So rushing like a lunatic from wherever she happened to be straight to the phone booth to retrieve her phone call, or more accurately, her lifeline to the outside world. These phone calls were the highlights of our mothers' days, and they tuned their ears in each time an announcement was made, hoping the phone call was for them. For us kids, the daily highlight was when the bakery truck and ice-cream truck would make their stops at our colony. We'd beg our mothers for a few quarters so we could get a cupcake or an ice-cream cone. For some reason, those bakery goods were the freshest and tastiest I've ever had.

Personally, I don't think my mother liked the whole bungalow colony arrangement. She was a free spirit and being cooped up like that all week was not for her, but as a child, I loved it. In the morning I would run out of the bungalow along with all the other kids in the colony, and we'd be busy from morning to night, returning to our bungalows just briefly when we got hungry. We all had bikes that we rode everywhere. We played baseball, punchball, volleyball, paddleball, and many other assorted sports. We picked blackberries, which grew in the neighboring bushes, as well as assorted wildflowers, and put them in soda bottles to decorate our bungalows. We caught frogs and built them ornate houses out of cardboard boxes complete with rocks for jumping, grass for sleeping, and a water bowl. I think their accommodations were nicer than ours. Somehow I would always manage to catch a really large frog, which would mysteriously disappear on me by the next day, and I would get into all sorts of arguments with the guys over my vanished frog.

We kids were always looking for ways to make a few bucks. We'd sell lemonade and iced tea, and when we got more ambitious we'd make these great carnivals where we would empty out anything we could find in our bungalows and create a booth out of it. Whatever we didn't have around our bungalows, we'd convince our mothers to buy for us. Some of our booths were:

- Count how many chocolate chips there were in a mouthful of marshmallow fluff.
- Bob for apples in a large bin of water.
- Reach into a box blindfolded and pick the bowl with the prize tickets. The other two bowls had ketchup and mustard.
- Shoot a lit candle with a water gun before your partner blew out his.

We even made a haunted house in an unused bungalow, where you could "feel the skeleton" (a mushy bowl of Vaseline), "hear the skeleton" (scary noises we'd howl at the blindfolded participant), and even "taste the skeleton's blood" (a disgusting drink we'd have them sample from everything in our refrigerator mixed together). At other times we'd put on cheesy magic shows that would often end with everyone demanding their money back. We were no Harry Houdinis performing out there, and the tricks were usually done in slow motion or without reading the instructions well enough, so that everyone could see exactly how the trick was done. Despite all this, I still have great memories of those carefree summer days. Sitting in my lounge chair or swaying in my hammock twenty years later, the memories of my bungalow colony years still come flooding back to me. I recall delightful summer days that would blend together like a song. You never knew where one day started and the next day ended until you were hauled into the family station wagon the day after Labor Day and found yourself wedged between a box or two as your family made their way back to the city.

Now, as I enjoy my backyard, taking in the cool summer night breeze, I relish those memories and those simpler times. Now it's about real life and real responsibilities—jobs, doctor's appointments, carpooling, setting up playdates, making sure your spouse has enough clean shirts in his closet. A part of me misses my younger, carefree self a whole lot. Not that I want to turn back the clock, but sometimes

I miss the less pressured times I experienced as a child, before the mortgages, bills, and schedules piled up. How I sometimes wish things were simpler now. I feel so blessed for everything I have, but with age comes wisdom, experience, responsibilities (there, I said that "r" word), and a certain knowledge that I can't go back. Rather, I can only savor the present and live life to its fullest, because soon the leaves will fall once again, and another season will have gone by, and another glorious summer will have slipped through my fingers. All I can do is savor the moment, look at each day as a chance to start fresh, and make the most out of it.